CONTENTS

PREFACE

When we write lyrics, we hold the pen of an artist. Whether we are writing for ourselves or for someone else, the objective is always the same—to cause a significant experience in the mind and heart of our listener. As writers, we have the power to determine the intensity of the experience we cause. Memorable songs connect artists to their audiences. Plots vary, but their ability to evoke laughter, elation, freedom, sorrow, regret, hope, or love remains the same. There is nothing more satisfying, in my opinion, than to reach listeners at their core—to gain access to the vaults of emotion by breathing life into a single chord, phrase, or melody. After all, emotions are the color of experience. They burn our lives into the depths of our memory. Without them, events—like songs—lack purpose.

There are many ways to write songs, from the deliberate use of time-tested techniques to simply letting inspiration guide the way. But even the best tools don't guarantee a great song, and inspiration is sometimes patchy. Some songs reach audiences regardless of their poor rhyme schemes, unparticular rhythms, and scant lyrical genius. So in the pages ahead, I am not attempting to write the conclusive book on songwriting. I am instead attempting to outline tools for writing with *intention*. Intention allows us to transfer our unique ideas eloquently to paper. It helps us to identify when a rhythm, a rhyme scheme, a chord, or a melody feels "off," and then put it right again. It helps us to learn what it is about our own artistic identity that makes our writing unique and marketable. Some songwriters can sing any lyric and make it sound convincing. If that's you, then you might have the rare talent of drawing an audience in simply through your voice, your musical style, your image, and even your aura. But if you're like me, you've got to work a little harder to gain an audience's attention. I've actually come to appreciate my inability to pass a cliché for an original thought, and I believe that very handicap has forced me to become a better writer.

I hear many writers and performing artists alike explain that they're not interested in writing for the mainstream market. But there is a reason why some song melodies are remembered longer, and why some lyrics seem to connect with our emotions stronger than other songs we hear. It is my belief that before we can write memorable songs outside the mainstream market, or "out of the box," so to speak, we've got to know what it means to write "inside the box." We also need to find out why the box has proved over and over again to be so effective. From punk, rock, reggae, and jazz to fusion, adult contemporary, pop, folk, and bebop, the tools that fuse the box together are all the same. The more we become aware of the tools available to us, the more flexible and effective we become as writers and artists.

ACKNOWLEDGMENTS

There are a few people I wish to thank who have played an irreplaceable role in the writing of this book. I thank Pat Pattison for his mentorship and his extreme insight into the craft of lyric writing. Without him, I would not be writing lyrics today. I thank Jimmy Kachulis for sharing his talent for making hit songwriting accessible to writers at all levels. I thank my parents, Mark and Jan Debe, for their unwavering encouragement and financial backing when times were rough. Let's not do that again, shall we? And I thank Jan Stolpe for his tough love, his vision, and his belief. Without them, I'd still be stuck in chapter 1.

Causing an Experience

THE ARTIST'S OBJECTIVE

You may not remember third-grade picture day in grammar school, but I remember it very well. I remember pulling at my navy-blue cotton jumper, the high collar scratching the skin on my neck to bright red. My long red hair was yanked up in a clip on top of my head, a last attempt to save what was left of a bad curling iron experience. My bangs sagged to the right like sunken-cake frosting, looping unnaturally under the weight of all the hairspray. I remember waiting in line while the children in front of me filed across the gym floor towards the black velvet curtain, where a man's voice lofted up and down on a pillow of air. He sounded much too happy to be there, insisting each of us say "cheesy cheesy pizza weezy" before snapping the bright strobe light. A moment later, his assistant quickly escorted us off stage and spit us back out into the hall towards our classroom. I couldn't wait to change back into the shorts and T-shirt I'd smuggled from home in my bookbag. The embarrassment of that Amish-inspired cotton number I was wearing was almost too much, but I knew the shame I would face at home if two weeks from now I came back with this year's photo in my dirty white T.

Yes, I remember that day very well, because of the strong feelings of embarrassment, frustration, and longing to escape. Now, maybe you always had great pictures, or maybe you never even had them taken at all. But through the honest and detailed description of my experience, I hope I've sparked an experience within you. Perhaps you smiled or your heart raced a little. Maybe you shuffled your feet uncomfortably across the carpet, nervously picked at a hole in your jeans, remembering a time when you felt similarly humiliated. Whatever your response, it was not the plot that got you there. It was the emotional connection caused by detail that for a moment, we shared.

In the pages ahead, we'll explore how it is not so important *what* we write about but *how* we write it. Any idea can succeed or fail in causing an experience with the listener. The effectiveness is not contained within the plot itself, but in the ability of the story to connect emotionally.

> Effectiveness is not contained within the plot, but in the ability of the story to connect emotionally.

In the chapters ahead, we'll use a ten-step process to gather ideas and present them in a way that causes an intense experience. We'll also expose angles of our own artistry that make each of us unique and inimitable as songwriters. So gather your pencil and notepad, and get ready to bare your soul.

MAKING PEOPLE CARE

Imagine a dimly lit club, a stage warming in the limelight, and the low drone of an audience wrapped up in their own Friday night concerns. You're about to perform one of your songs. You walk on stage, guitar in hand, take your place in front of the microphone, and urge your right hand to begin strumming. Eyes divert from their shadowed tables and begin to size up your haircut, your loose T-shirt, and your faded jeans. You sing your first line, "Baby baby, when you left, it hurt so bad." You keep strumming, gaining momentum as you sing the second line, "What did I ever do to make you so mad?" By this point, the initial shiver of walking out in front of fifty strangers has run its course, and you're feeling pretty good about yourself. But line-by-line, eyes return to their tables and the dull murmur rises again as conversations pick up where they left off. By the time you finish your first chorus, you might as well be practicing alone in your living room. So, what happened?

In order to care, your audience has got to feel something. Whatever that feeling is, it's got to be stronger than the smell of the burger and fries just laid on the table in front of them. Somewhere between the anticipation of your first note and the end of the first chorus, the audience lost interest. The song failed to convince the listener to care enough to pay attention. You may think, "But I'm singing about my last breakup! My heart was torn in two! What more do they want?" Quite frankly, they want you and your true story. The trouble is, there is a disconnect between the words you're singing and the emotion you mean to convey. The audience doesn't believe you're giving them the whole truth. They don't feel you're giving them you. But if you describe how when she left, you crumbled to the floor, the pit of your stomach burning, and hot tears welling up in the lids of your eyes as you buried your face in your clammy hands . . . then, they might actually pay some attention. The listener's experience matches the intensity of the event. And if it really wasn't that intense in the first place, why are you bothering to sing a song about it?

You might consider these two ideas when evaluating your connection with the audience.

First, determine the experience you wish to cause. Are you getting glazed looks or intense concentration? Is there a constant conversation going on in the room, or are eyes and ears hanging on your next lines? If you're not sure what experience you wish to cause, then chances are, you're not causing one. Take an emotional inventory. Are you connecting with your listeners or providing background music to their busy lives?

Second, get real. Once you can put into words the experience you wish for your audience, you can begin taking steps towards recreating that experience. Memorable songs cause intense experiences. Unmemorable songs don't cause any experience at all. Consider whether you stay in the realm of generalities at the cost of connection. Then ask yourself, what would I lose by being more specific?

In order to care, your audience has got to feel something. They've got to feel what it's like to be you in that moment. Telling them to care won't make them care. You've got to allow them to feel what you feel, to see what you see, to come to believe what you've come to believe.

Let's look at a few different approaches to capturing our audience's attention through our lyrics. I hope this information will inspire you to believe it's not so critical *what* you write about, but *how* you write about it. Let's begin tapping into that valuable perspective that is uniquely and solely your own.

CHAPTER 2

Exposing the Artist Perspective

BUILDING BLOCKS OF CONNECTION

> *"Object writing is writing from your senses. Its whole purpose is to connect your writing to what you see, touch, taste, smell, and hear; to the way your body responds—increased breathing, heart rate, pulse, muscle tension; and, finally, to your sense of movement. It provides your songs with their pictures and experiences."*
>
> —PAT PATTISON, *WRITING BETTER LYRICS*

Sense-bound writing will be the foundation of all connection throughout this book. This explosion of thought is crucial to getting to the heart of what connects within our idea and expressing it vividly and efficiently to our listener. Daily object writing is a great way to become skilled at using sense-bound language.

For the purpose of coming up with song lyrics, I use a type of object writing called *destination writing*. Destination writing is sense-bound free writing directed at a place, a person, or a time instead of an object. The key to both destination writing and object writing is involving the senses of touch, taste, smell, sight, sound, and also movement. When those senses are involved, the writing springs to life.

A good way to visualize what we're doing when we destination-write is to imagine ourselves as a camera lens. The closer we zoom in, the more detail we see. The bulk of our writing will be spent zoomed in so close that we will see the very pores and veins of a place, person, or time.

Zoomed In

Zoomed Out

But once in a while, we'll also zoom out and comment on the landscape and big picture. Let's imagine we're destination writing about a place, such as a busy sidewalk in New York City. Zoomed in, we might describe "handbags slapping against passing elbows and the rhythm of legs like windmills propelling bodies through a mass of driven faces . . ." But zoomed out on the same scenario, we might write, "A sidewalk full of people trying to get somewhere, all worrying about their schedules, their relationships, and scurrying for direction in life." Detail allows our listener to step into our shoes, know what we know, and feel how we feel. Too little detail and we generalize the experience, losing intensity. Too much detail and we run the risk of delving so deep into the abyss of description that we only emerge with some thoughtful poetry.

So what does destination writing actually look like on paper, and how do we tap into the depth of detail we need when we're writing? I find it helpful to list the senses at the top of the page, before I begin writing. These six keys of connection keep us focused, and our writing poised for a powerful experience.

> **SIX KEYS OF CONNECTION:**
> 1. Taste
> 2. Touch
> 3. Sight
> 4. Sound
> 5. Smell
> 6. Movement

In the destination writing below, pay special attention to the sense each detail describes. Consider how describing an experience in terms of our senses allows us to imagine and become part of the event itself.

KEYWORD: `Airport`

I slumped down on the cool plastic chair in front of gate B14. The crack in the seat exhaled as the weight of my duffel bag sank like a barbell on top. As I looked around, the woman next to me was reading a worn romance novel, her bifocals resting on the ball of her nose, her wrists poised on her lap as she rigidly held the book upright. The man beside her glanced nervously around, patting his right shirt pocket for cigarettes and murmuring expletives as he fought with the button that kept him from his habitual relief. The small of my back ached as I shifted in my chair. I combed my hair with my fingers, feeling the futility of sifting through my bag for a brush. I hadn't showered for two days, being trapped on a bus, then a train, then another bus, until finally I was spit out in the hustle of an airport crowd, misshapen and generally disgusted with the lines at security. The intercom rang through the terminal, muffled and washed out by the buzz of travelers. My nose caught the pungent odor of a hamburger and french fries...

Each sentence in this paragraph contains critical details that provide the reader with an experience rather than just plot. At this point you may be thinking, "It sounds good, but I just can't write like that." Well, I'm going to let you in on a secret. Ready? You can. The answer lies in tiny powerhouse words that mean the difference between a bored audience and one that is hanging on your every word. Let me illustrate by rewriting the same paragraph, replacing one particular group of powerhouses called **verbs**, with a more generic substitution:

```
I sat down on the cool plastic chair in front of
gate B14. There was a crack in the seat and the
weight of my duffel bag was like a barbell on
top. As I looked around, the woman next to me was
reading a worn romance novel, her bifocals on the
ball of her nose, her wrists on her lap as she
rigidly held the book upright. The man beside her
looked nervously around, touching his right shirt
pocket for cigarettes and speaking expletives as he
tried the button that kept him from his habitual
relief. The small of my back hurt as I moved in my
chair. I combed my hair with my fingers, feeling
the futility of going through my bag for a brush.
I hadn't showered for two days, being trapped on a
bus, then a train, then another bus until finally
I was let out in the hustle of an airport crowd,
unhappy with the lines at security. The intercom
went through the terminal, muffled and washed out
by the noise of travelers. My nose smelled the
pungent odor of a hamburger and french fries...
```

You might feel that the paragraph has lost some of its ability to cause a strong experience. The intensity of the original verbs certainly helped to garner some valuable attention. But at this point, it still has some redeeming qualities found in another tiny powerhouse, the **adjectives**. Let's experiment by deleting the adjectives and even some adverbs that color our everyday nouns:

I sat down on the chair in front of the gate. There was a crack in the seat and the weight of my duffel bag sat like a barbell on top. As I looked around, the woman next to me was reading a romance novel, her bifocals on her nose, her wrists on her lap as she held the book upright. The man beside her looked around, touching his right shirt pocket for cigarettes and speaking expletives as he tried the button that kept him from his relief. The small of my back hurt as I moved in my chair. I combed my hair with my fingers, feeling the futility of going through my bag for a brush. I hadn't showered for two days, being trapped on a bus, then a train, then another bus until finally I was out in the airport crowd, unhappy with the lines at security. The intercom went through the terminal, over the noise of travelers. My nose smelled the odor of a hamburger and french fries...

At this point, my destination writing is really suffering. It seems that all that is left are basic plot ideas. The experience caused by this paragraph is far weaker than the experience caused by the original. From this exercise, we can draw a few conclusions about what turns a plot into an experience and how much attention we can expect from our audience:

> Experience is caused through verbs, adjectives, and adverbs. The *way* the idea is written matters *more* than the idea itself.

Ideas in themselves are neither good nor bad. They're just simply ideas. It's what's in between those ideas that is the secret to connection. Generalized detail causes generalized emotion. Specific detail causes strong, specific emotion. You decide what you want your audience to remember more—their burger and fries, or you.

EXERCISE 2.1. Getting Sense Bound

Practice using your senses to describe the destination keyword listed below. Beside each question, describe the situation in as much detail as possible.

KEYWORD: **Bus Station**

Taste   Touch   Sight   Smell   Sound   Movement

On what are you standing or sitting?

_____

_____

_____

What do you smell?

_____

_____

_____

What do you taste?

_____

_____

_____

What around you is moving?

_____

_____

_____

What do you hear?

_____

_____

_____

What clothes, jewelry, and hairdo are you wearing?

_____

_____

_____

What are you feeling and thinking?

_____

_____

_____

Look back over your descriptions from this exercise. Compare your verbs and adjectives with those listed below. If you find duplicates, you may not be getting specific enough. Try replacing those generic placeholders with some alternates and compare the results. Also, locate any nouns standing alone without the help of descriptive adjectives and give them a friend.

Generic Verbs, Adjectives, and Nouns:

Good, bad, food, walking, sitting, sad, smell, taste, hear, big, small, pants, shoes, shirt, dress, earrings, necklace, suit and tie, smile, face

EXERCISE 2.2. Generating Powerhouse Verbs

In the list below, you'll find common verbs and adjectives used in everyday conversation. To the right of each generic word is a list of specific words that can be swapped out for our one- or two-syllable sleeping pill. For help coming up with these lists, just look to your thesaurus. Every time you feel yourself reverting back to generalized action words, refer to the smorgasbord of synonyms. Try filling in your own ideas in the blanks below and complete the list.

Walk: wander, stroll, march, step, strut, shuffle

Put: lay, set, store, place, plant, fix

Said: utter, breathe, blurt, pronounce, stammer, stutter, mouth, jabber, muffle

Shine: glint, glare, sparkle, radiate, shimmer, flash, blaze, beam, flicker

Realize: discover, find, determine, unravel, interpret, unearth, disclose, recognize

Color: _____

_____

Describe: _____

_____

Want: _____

_____

Think: _____

_____

Grow: _____

_____

Love: _____

_____

Jump: _____

_____

EXERCISE 2.3. Daily Destination Writing

Six minutes is all you need to begin destination writing. Reserve a notebook especially for your lyric gems, and set a timer or watch the clock so you don't run over. Using the list of places, people, and times in appendix A, let your stream of consciousness flow over the paper. Remember to post the six keys of connection somewhere that you can refer to them often while you write.

WRITING FROM THE SUBJECT

Much of our destination writing will flow from a keyword place or "where." But sometimes, you'll find that a person or time as your keyword will yield some great material. Whether you're writing from bus station, TV evangelist, or just after midnight, you'll use the same six keys of connection to tap into that great sense-bound language.

I'd like to take this opportunity to tell you about my Aunt Louise. If your family is anything like mine, you'll understand that after Thanksgiving dinner, she's got her hands in the dishwater while her husband of thirty-nine years retires his bulging belly to the living-room easy chair. Now, let's say my Aunt Louise is the keyword that sparks my next destination writing. There are a few ways I can approach this subject, so I'll just start from the shoes of Aunt Louise:

KEYWORD: `Aunt Louise`

```
I gazed down at my dry, rough fingers swishing in the
murky, lukewarm dishwater. They weren't attractive
anymore, I thought. The hands of a working girl.
A thin film of grease floated over the surface of
the water as tiny soapsuds popped and dissipated
into nothingness. The drain acted like a funnel,
sucking small doses of the particled water with a
wheezy slurring sound. I smiled as the laughter
from the living room drifted under the door into
the kitchen. Family meant everything to me, the
kids, the grandkids, the exes, and the in-laws. To
take care of them was my joy in life.
```

We can see the powerhouses at work with specific verbs and adjectives like swishing, wheezy, slurring, and popped. Those details allow our listener to experience this event rather than just watch it from a distance. But there is something else at work here. You may have noticed that instead of writing about Aunt Louise, I became Aunt Louise. Using "I" instead of "she" provided an intimacy that may not have otherwise occurred. This is called first person point of view. When destination writing from "who," it is often helpful to write from first person point of view, assuming the role of the main character of the song.

> When destination writing from "who," it is helpful to assume the role of the main character of the song.

That way, the details have the opportunity to become as intimate as possible and the experience as authentic as it can be. Later on, we can change our point of view, if we can't see how Aunt Louise would make the top-ten list for our next record.

But there is another way to write in first person without taking on the role of Aunt Louise. I could write from the position of an outsider. Maybe I'm a relative, a friend, a lost love, or even a stranger passing by her kitchen window. Whoever I am, I'm still writing with "I." The details are given stronger purpose and the emotions made more intense because of my intimate relationship to the story. Distancing myself from my main character risks weakening the intensity of the emotion I am able to feel. This doesn't mean that only songs written in first person point of view succeed in relating strong experiences. But what we're trying to do in this stage of our writing is become intimately acquainted with our story. If we're not specific with what emotion we're trying to evoke, the feeling the audience experiences will also be unspecific. Later on, we can play with perspective, or use Aunt Louise only as a metaphor and a means for conveying our ultimate chorus message.

Let's use the same keyword, only this time, take on the role of an outsider:

KEYWORD: Aunt Louise

Her hands delicately drew the tattered washcloth over the pan, dunking the griddle halfway into the dishwater before drawing it up again and inspecting what was left of the grease. Wisps of hair fell over her eyes and she brushed them away behind her ears. I thought I could hear her humming, and out of the corner of my eye I saw her hips sway a little. As I cleared the rest of the dishes from the table, I thought about how many Thanksgivings we'd shared at her house. Even when things weren't great at my own home, she always managed to make this feel like the place I belonged and the family that couldn't live without me.

The description is just as intimate and the connection just as believable, but my role has simply moved outside of Aunt Louise.

Let's say I'd like to write a song to go along with that fantastic video collage your cousin Hernando had been whipping up for your aunt and uncle's fiftieth wedding anniversary. The experience I want to create is one of nostalgia and respect. Instead of acting as a main character in the song, I'd like to focus the tune around the happy couple.

KEYWORD: **Aunt Louise**

She swished her hands in the murky dishwater and felt for the ratted green sponge she used to scrub the dried gravy from the griddle. From the living room floated a hefty chuckle from the gut of her husband of more years than she could remember. She smiled to herself, as the drone of the TV filled the house with a warmth and glow that surrounded them for nearly all their married life. It wasn't always so easy. She examined her fingernails, soft and opaque as if she had rubbed her hands in chalk dust. The smell of lemon and chlorine drifted from the dishwasher and she could almost taste the dry heat escaping from the rinse cycle into the air. She drew tap water from the kitchen sink and lit the gas under the teapot. It sparked and hissed as droplets dripped from the bottom edge of the ceramic pot down into the elements…

When writing from "who," it helps to imagine an action being performed. For example, "middle-aged woman" might not give you many ideas. But, "middle-aged woman painting in the nude" would certainly arouse some questions. Adding an action helps us to get more specific with our details.

Different roles yield different details. In all roles, the details we choose to include are the result of the intimate portrayal of the experience. Writing from "who" as well as "where" can lead to song ideas we never imagined we had. And who doesn't want more ideas?

WRITING FROM "WHEN"

There is one more type of keyword we can use as the topic for our destination writing. We can use a time or "when" to spark specific details and content. Whether or not we're aware of it, "when" always plays a role in our destination writing. In the case of "airport," "when" was defined as a moment probably no longer than a minute while waiting and watching others around me. For Aunt Louise, "when" was after dinner while doing dishes. The interesting thing about "when" is that the shorter the time that passes, the more specific the details we can provide. Conversely, the longer the span of time, the more generalized the details end up being. Remember that connection with our audience depends on our ability to cause an experience. Generalizations do very little to grab and hold attention, so I'll say it again:

> The narrower the time frame, the more specific the detail.

Imagine you and I meet face to face for the first time. After you introduce yourself, you politely ask how I am. Now, deep down, I know that it's simply a pleasantry, and you're not really interested in hearing about my dog barking at 3 A.M., the hot water heater that always seems to provide only enough water for my upstairs neighbor to take a long relaxing dip, and the shirt I intended on wearing this morning tossed in a heap in the dirty laundry. No, I'd probably just say, "Fine, thank you, and you?" The point is, to truly expect you to understand and experience how I was feeling, I'd have to go into greater detail. Grazing the surface of those events forces you to stay on the outside of my experience.

Now, let's say we knew each other very well, and you could sense that I was unusually upset. Instead of bombarding you with the highlights of my whole night, I'd choose a moment that captures the true frustration I experienced:

"I can't concentrate and my thoughts are scattered, now that my new puppy responds to every thump and twitter outside my bedroom walls. When I glanced at the clock last night, it was just after 3 A.M. My bed sheets were rumpled from his claws shuffling the cotton into a thick ball before he'd thrust his nose underneath and snort. Then he'd perk his ears and tail straight out like a dart, and catapult off the bed. In Stevie Wonder style, he'd sway his head side to side and bark aimlessly up towards the window."

At this point, I have given you enough detail that you could relate to and imagine my frustration. That experience causes connection in a way that grazing the surface of more numerous events never could.

We can think of time and detail as a cycle, each one feeding the other. The more specific the time, the more convincing the detail. In other words, the more details, the less time that passes.

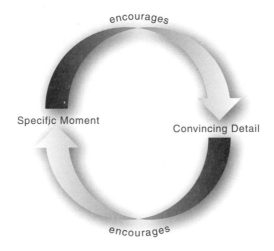

When we talk about the amount of time that passes, we're not talking about the plot of the whole song. Many effective songs describe events that take place from childhood to adulthood, or before a relationship to after the relationship has ended. What we're interested in is identifying what happens within a single song section. Those details are the fruits of our destination writing. They are the result of a specific time, person, or place.

LISTENING SUGGESTIONS

Sting, "Stolen Car (Take Me Dancing)"
Joni Mitchell, "A Case of You"
Melissa Etheridge, "All American Girl"
Bob Dylan, "Big Yellow Taxi"

Chapter Summary

1. Destination writing is stream-of-consciousness writing involving the senses and directed around a keyword place, person, or time.
2. The six keys of connection are taste, touch, sight, smell, sound, and movement.
3. Experience is conveyed through verbs, adjectives, and adverbs.
4. *How* we write matters far more than *what* we write.
5. The shorter the time that passes, the more convincing the detail. The longer the time that passes, the more generalized and less convincing the detail.
6. What experience do you want to cause for your listener?

CHAPTER 3

Two Types of Detail

HIDDEN CLUES OF DESTINATION WRITING

Now that you've introduced daily destination writing into your creative process, let's explore how we can use these bursts of detail to compose song lyrics. Reading back over the first destination writing on "airport," we can categorize each phrase of our writing into two different types of detail. This categorization will help to organize the subject matter and recombine it into song form.

There are two types of detail: external and internal. **External detail** describes the actions or objects surrounding the main character of the song. The detail is concrete and often provokes an image in the mind of our listener. **Internal detail** describes the thoughts and emotions within the main character of the song. The detail is abstract, sometimes metaphorical, and does not provoke an image in the mind of our listener.

External Detail	Internal Detail
• Actions and objects surrounding the main character	• Thoughts and emotions within the main character
• Concrete	• Abstract
• Provokes an image	• Does not provoke an image
	• Often metaphorical

To better understand these two types of detail, let's refer to the "Airport" destination writing. Each sentence is made up of phrases. Phrases can be two or more words long and will often consist of an adjective and noun, an adverb and noun, or a verb and noun. Now don't worry, you won't need to have an in-depth study of grammar to determine the different types of detail. All you need to be able to do is identify and isolate those groups of words that create these phrases.

Phrase = Noun + Adjective/Adverb/Verb

Sometimes a useful detail will only be one word—a specific noun or verb that helps to describe the mood and action of the surrounding detail. In the paragraph below, I've underlined potentially useful phrases and words in my destination writing on "Airport."

KEYWORD: **Airport**

I <u>slumped down</u> on the <u>cool plastic chair</u> in front of <u>gate B14</u>. The <u>crack</u> in the <u>seat exhaled</u> as the <u>weight</u> of my <u>duffel bag</u> <u>sank like a barbell</u> on top. As I looked around, the <u>woman next to me</u> was <u>reading</u> a <u>worn romance novel</u>, her <u>bifocals resting</u> on the <u>ball of her nose</u>, her <u>wrists resting</u> on her <u>lap</u> as she <u>rigidly held the book</u> <u>upright</u>. The <u>man beside her</u> <u>glanced nervously</u> around, <u>patting</u> his <u>right shirt pocket for cigarettes</u> and <u>murmuring expletives</u> as he <u>fought with the button</u> that kept him from his habitual relief. The <u>small of my back ached</u> as I <u>shifted in my chair</u>. I <u>combed my hair</u> with my <u>fingers</u>, feeling the futility of <u>sifting through my bag</u> for a <u>brush</u>. I hadn't showered for two days, being <u>trapped</u> on a <u>bus</u>, then a <u>train</u>, then another bus until finally being <u>spit out</u> in the <u>hustle</u> of an <u>airport crowd</u>, <u>misshapen</u> and generally disgusted with the <u>lines at security</u>. The <u>intercom rang</u> through the <u>terminal</u>, <u>muffled and washed out</u> by the <u>buzz of travelers</u>. My <u>nose</u> caught the <u>pungent odor</u> of a <u>hamburger and french fries</u>...

Notice that I underlined single words and groups of words, avoiding conjunctions and prepositions that connected phrases to each other. (For a list of prepositions and conjunctions, refer to appendix B.) My goal here is to grab only the essence of the phrase, retaining my original idea in the smallest grouping possible. In later steps, you'll see how this streamlines the process, eliminating clutter while allowing more flexibility when recombining the phrases into lyrical lines.

You may also notice that there are a few phrases that I have not underlined. "As I looked around," "that kept him from his habitual relief," "generally disgusted," and "then another bus" are phrases I have intentionally left blank. The reason is that the essence of those phrases is simply commentary. They are evaluations made by the main character, myself, about the events happening around me. They express thoughts or emotions and are therefore internal details. As you may have suspected, the underlined phrases are external details. They describe the actions and objects surrounding the main character and evoke an image instead of a thought or feeling. When determining if a phrase is external or internal, it is sometimes helpful to hold it against these two discerning questions:

> Does the phrase describe what's going on around the main character?

If so, then the detail is external.

> Does the phrase describe what's going on within the heart or mind of the main character?

If so, then the detail is internal.

Without the help of external details, internal details lie flat and remain two-dimensional. We saw the effects of that in chapter 1 with "Baby, when you left, it hurt so bad." As lyrics, these lines result in bored, fidgeting audiences who don't remember our songs or us. But when we precede those internal detail lines with external detail, the thoughts and emotions come alive like a stained glass window in a burst of sunlight.

Now that we have identified the two types of detail within the destination writing, we can list them in two columns to get an overview of their combination potential.

Very simply, we'll transfer the phrases exactly as we've underlined them into an External column on the left and an Internal column on the right:

External		Internal
Slumped down	Airport crowd	Kept him from his
Cool plastic chair	Misshapen	habitual relief
Gate B14	Wrists poised	I hadn't showered for
Crack	Lap	two days
Seat exhaled	Rigidly held the book	Generally disgusted
Weight	upright	Then another bus
Duffel bag	Man beside her	
Glanced nervously	Lines at security	
Patting	Intercom rang	
Right shirt pocket	Terminal	
Cigarettes	Muffled and washed	
Murmuring expletives	out	
Fought with the	Buzz of travelers	
button	Nose	
Small of my back	Pungent odor	
Ached	Hamburger and	
Shifted in my chair	french fries	
Combed my hair	Fingers	
Spit out	Sifting through my	
Hustle	bag	
Ball of her nose	Brush	
Woman next to me	Trapped on a bus	
Sank like a barbell	Train	
	Worn romance novel	
	Bifocals resting	

Sometimes, external detail can become internal, as it is lifted out of the destination-writing paragraph. This happens when the phrase has been cut too drastically and the essence of the meaning is distilled. An example of this is "trapped." I can either move the word into the Internal column and consider it a feeling or thought, or I can add back in the rest of the phrase "on a bus" to complete the image and leave it in the External column.

When you first begin destination writing, you may find you have a longer internal detail list than external detail list. But with practice and remembering to stay focused on those six keys of connection, you'll begin to throw more weight on the external column.

If you find you're having difficulty discerning whether a phrase is external or internal, don't lose heart. Refer back to the two discerning questions, and then ask yourself whether the phrase produces a strong image, or if it is more abstract or metaphorical. A phrase here and there that slips through the cracks and resides in the wrong column won't mean sudden death to your lyric. As we continue the process, your ability to identify the usefulness of each phrase will sharpen.

With our destination writing separated into two columns, we can now see the external and internal details clearly. Here's where the magic happens. Listen carefully, because this can get so exciting that you'll find yourself foregoing necessary chores and hygiene habits like cleaning out last month's leftovers from the fridge, feeding Rover, and maybe even flossing.

The external column is the majority of material that will become the verse content. It is our immediate tool for connection and the secret weapon in banishing boredom from our audiences.

The internal column is the material that will aerate the verse and provide purpose. It jumps to the heart of the matter, summing up why the song is worth writing and listening to.

> The external column will become the verse content.
> The internal column will aerate the verse while providing purpose.

Using these guidelines as the compass for our song direction will help us to write a section that sounds as riveting and also as natural as possible. So how do we know what sounds natural and what doesn't? Well, first we can use our ears and instincts. But we also have another tool called "weight." No, don't put down that jelly doughnut. When we talk about the weight of a section, we're talking about the amount of essential information that is present and the pace at which that essential information is relayed.

Weight = Essential Information + Pace

Read aloud the two verses below. Notice how the first section is laden with detail, while the second is light and more generic.

Verse:
The mud from our shoes
left prints on the floor
and the rain on the stoop
spilled in as it poured
the shingles were flapping
the windows were clapping
but we stayed inside safe and warm

Verse:
Baby we could say what we feel
and do what we say
remember why we're together
and look forward to forever
then nothing can stop us
nothing can tear us apart
with these two hearts

A heavily weighted section requires intense concentration for the listener to process. A lightly weighted section requires little concentration and therefore receives little concentration to process. Both extremes can result in a loss of connection. A balance between these two extremes is the most desirable weight for a section. Sometimes, we can feel instinctually that the scales are dipping to one side or the other. Those instincts are a valuable gauge, and with the tools of the next chapter, we'll learn how to not only identify heavy or flimsy areas but also fix them.

EXERCISE 3.1. Distinguishing Detail

Circle E for external or I for internal next to each phrase below. When in doubt, apply the two discerning questions presented in this chapter.

1.	E or I	Consider me gone
2.	E or I	Crisp, brittle oak leaves
3.	E or I	Only the lonely
4.	E or I	Coarsely woven, tattered quilt
5.	E or I	Thin black eraser crumbs
6.	E or I	There's no one else like you
7.	E or I	I thought about how much I missed you
8.	E or I	The door stuck slightly
9.	E or I	Cold rush of air-conditioned air
10.	E or I	But you're not
11.	E or I	Draperies flecked with grease
12.	E or I	This would all be bearable if you were here

Answers: 1. I 2. E 3. I 4. E 5. E 6. I 7. I 8. E 9. E 10. I 11. E 12. I

EXERCISE 3.2. Applying Identities

Practice identifying external and internal phrases in your own destination writing. Underline the external details, excluding prepositions and conjunctions. Leave internal phrases blank.

EXERCISE 3.3. Creating Columns

Practice listing your external and internal phrases in their appropriate columns. Take a clean sheet of paper, and draw a line down the center, marking the left column "external" and the right column "internal." Transfer your underlined and blank phrases from exercise 3.2 onto the new sheet.

LISTENING SUGGESTIONS
Counting Crows, "Mr. Jones"
The Eagles, "Hotel California"
Tori Amos, "Winter"
Faith Hill, "On a Bus to St. Cloud"

Chapter Summary

1. The two types of detail are **external** and **internal**.
2. External detail describes what's going on around the main character. Internal details describe the thoughts and feelings of the main character himself.
3. A phrase is a noun plus an adjective, adverb, or verb.
4. External details make up the bulk of verse content. Internal details aerate the verse while providing purpose.
5. Weight determines the amount of concentration our listener needs to process the song detail.

CHAPTER 4

Rhyme

ROLLER-SKATING FOR MATCHES

In the sixth grade, I took a few field trips to the local roller-skating rink with my brother and a few others whose moms remembered to turn in the consent forms. Smashed peanut-butter sandwiches and a token bag of carrots in our knapsacks, we'd skate until just past dinnertime before loading the bus to ride back home. It was indeed a special treat. But I also remember the terrifying entrance of a slow song pumping through the tinny speakers over the rink. That usually meant there was a humiliating game of snowball ahead, where pubescent boys would line up on one side of the oval and pretend the whole thing was silly, and blushing girls would rest their arms against the opposite wall wondering if and when they would be plucked from the row to dance. Well, I'll spare you the description of the horror on the faces of those left standing along the walls, but I will use the whole ordeal as a metaphor for rhyme.

Imagine our columned phrases represented the girls and boys lined up alongside their respective walls. Our job is to find rhyme pairs for our lyrics both between and within these columns. Let's use the columns from "Airport" and see some of the rhymes that exist.

External		Internal
Slumped down	Airport crowd	Kept him from his
Cool plastic chair	Misshapen	habitual relief
Gate B14	Wrists poised	I hadn't showered for
Crack	Lap	two days
Seat exhaled	Rigidly held the book	Generally disgusted
Weight	upright	Then another bus
Duffel bag	Man beside her	
Glanced nervously	Lines at security	
Patting	Intercom rang	
Right shirt pocket	Terminal	
Cigarettes	Muffled and washed	
Murmuring expletives	out	
Fought with the	Buzz of travelers	
button	Nose	
Small of my back	Pungent odor	
Ached	Hamburger and	
Shifted in my chair	french fries	
Combed my hair	Fingers	
Spit out	Sifting through my	
Hustle	bag	
Ball of her nose	Brush	
Woman next to me	Trapped on a bus	
Sank like a barbell	Train	
	Worn romance novel	
	Bifocals resting	

Comparing some of the sounds out loud, I can come up with a list of rhymes like this:

Rhyme Pairs:
Slumped d**own**/spit **out**
Cool plastic ch**air**/combed my h**air**
Small of my back **ach**ed/duffel b**ag**
w**eigh**t/seat ex**hale**d

I can also look within the phrases for rhymes instead of limiting myself to just the ends of the phrases listed:

gate/two days
murmuring expletives/spit
crack/small of my back
duffel/button
seat/habitual relief
disgusted/button
nervously/murmuring
bus/nervous

You might be looking at this list and thinking, "I didn't know that nervously and murmuring were rhymes." Strictly speaking, they are not. But rhyme as it pertains to lyric can push the envelope, riding on rhythms and the ebb and flow of musical phrasing to convince our ears of a connection. Sometimes a loose connection is more desirable, as we'll explore in the next chapter.

For now, practice stretching your imagination and pairing up your girls and boys, external and internal, until you arrive at a list of possible matches. With so many options before we even begin to write our lyric, we find ourselves in a unique position. Ideas we would have searched long and hard for are now right in front of us. Rhymes that may never have surfaced are now available. Best of all, our lyric is positioned to sound natural and utterly original.

EXERCISE 4.1.   Finding Rhyme Pairs

Using one of your daily destination writings, identify as many rhymes as you can from your external and internal columns. List them in the spaces below.

TO RHYME OR NOT TO RHYME

This is your chance to use the good education on rhyming you received in your preschool years. Some of the first rhymes you probably learned were "cat" and "hat," "see" and "bee," and "car" and "star." That rhyme type is called perfect rhyme, and requires that both the vowel sounds and the ending consonant sounds match. Sticking to that rhyme type alone pretty much ensures we'll never be able to finish a line with "orange."

But what someone failed to tell us is that there is a whole world of rhyme outside of cats and hats. That's where other rhyme types come in. They allow us to express ourselves exactly as we would in natural conversation. And as you remember, our connection with our listener depends on our ability to create a strong, believable experience.

There are five rhyme types you will find yourself using over and over in your lyrics. For more detailed background on these types, refer to *Songwriting: Essential Guide to Rhyming* by Pat Pattison (Berklee Press, 1991).

For our purposes, we'll talk about rhyme in its ability to create a believable experience. Sometimes, a perfect rhyme does not limit content. In other words, sometimes we get lucky, and the perfect rhyme conveys exactly the meaning we intend. But other times, we are guilty of choosing a word for its ability to rhyme rather than its content. What results is a feeling of contrivance. The audience may not be able to put into words why they emotionally check out, but it is often because they are suddenly paying less attention to what we're saying and more attention to "how" we're saying it. Choosing a word based solely on its ability to rhyme rarely pays off.

So how do we know when we're hitting the mark and when we're taking long shots? One way is to consider the amount of closure a rhyme provides. Closure is the degree of perfection to which the rhyme causes finality. Perfect rhyme (well, sell) provides the most closure. Consonance rhyme, described below (bag, log), provides the least closure. The strongest degree of perfection is sometimes the barest giveaway of poor content. If the rhyme appears too obvious, the listener is more likely to doubt that what we're saying is true. The same can go for very loose rhyme as well. If the match is too awkward, it may draw attention away from what we're saying and onto how we're saying it. So the answer lies in our ability to hear the difference. As with all rhyme, the beginning consonants must be different or it would qualify as **identity**, where we feel an awkward repetition instead of closure.

Type 1. Perfect

The strongest degree of closure is perfect rhyme. Perfect rhyme means that both the ending consonants (if any) and stressed vowel sounds of two words match exactly.

Examples of perfect rhyme are: well, sell; chase, face; saw, flaw; form, dorm.

Type 2. Family

The second strongest degree of closure is family rhyme. Family rhyme occurs when the stressed vowel sounds match exactly and the ending consonant sounds are closely linked. Family rhymes are like cousins of perfect rhymes.

Some examples of family rhyme are: wet, deck; dame, grain; float, yoke; math, pass.

Type 3. Additive/Subtractive

The third strongest degree of closure is additive/subtractive rhyme. Like its name, additive rhyme means that a consonant ending has been added to the matching vowel sounds. Subtractive rhyme means that a consonant ending has been deleted from the matching vowel sounds.

Examples of additive rhyme are: stow, hope; year, feared; down, found.

Examples of subtractive rhyme are: bake, stay; shout, now; roll, know.

Type 4. Assonance

The fourth strongest degree of closure is assonance rhyme. Assonance rhyme requires that the stressed vowel sounds match, but that the ending consonant sounds be different. Keep in mind that assonance can easily become family rhyme if the ending consonant sounds are related.

Examples of assonance rhyme are: rope, known; straight, fame; still, grip.

Type 5. Consonance

The weakest degree of closure is consonance rhyme. Consonance means that the vowel sounds do not match, but the ending consonants are the same. You can think of it as the opposite of assonance rhyme.

Examples of consonance rhyme are: bag, log; ground, bond; stood, wade; sock, back.

Sometimes the pair won't strictly adhere to any of these descriptions. "Nervously"and "murmuring" have rhymed beginning sounds of "ner-" and "mur-," but the ending sounds differ. According to our definitions, that might seem most like assonance rhyme. The bottom line is that sometimes the final decision comes down to our most valuable tool: our ears.

EXERCISE 4.2. The Five Rhyme Types

For each word provided, supply a rhyme using each of the five rhyme types.

	TYPE 1 PERFECT	TYPE 2 FAMILY	TYPE 3 ADDITIVE	TYPE 3 SUBTRACTIVE	TYPE 4 ASSONANCE	TYPE 5 CONSONANCE
WRONG						
RUN						
CONFUSE						
LIGHT						
TRACK						
BOAT						

STRUCTURE AND SCHEME

When it comes to rhyme, there are two other important factors in determining a match and the amount of closure the match provides. They are:

> Position the rhyme holds in the line.
> Position the rhyme holds in the section.

Let me illustrate each with the lyrics below:

"When She Thinks About Leavin'"

The TV is flashing
and blurred in the background
as she clears the plates off the table
And sighs at the dishes
then slips out a picture
taped by the cupboard door handle

The section you've just read is made up of two groups of three lines. The rhyme scheme in the first half mirrors the rhyme scheme in the second half. When two lines rhyme, they are represented with the same letter. Lines that do not rhyme with any other in the section are notated with an "X." Upon looking at this section, it can be difficult to tell where the rhymes occur. But if we are open to loose rhyme—those that are similar in sound but not exact—we can begin to see the rhyme scheme emerge that our ears already hear:

The TV is flashing	A
and blurred in the background	A
as she clears the plates off the table	B
And sighs at the dishes	C
then slips out a picture	C
taped by the cupboard door handle	B

Even though lines 1 and 2 are a very loose assonance rhyme, they provide a degree of connection, weaving the lyric together with a common thread. The same rhyme type occurs in lines 4 and 5, another loose assonance rhyme continuing the pattern. Finally, line 6 closes down the whole section with a consonance rhyme for "table."

So why is closure so important? Or in other words, what would happen if this lyric were written with perfect rhyme giving more closure? How about if there were no rhyme at all, giving no closure? And how would it affect the overall believability of the section and the intensity of the experience it causes? To answer these questions, let's take a look at the section rewritten with perfect rhyme in exactly the same positions as the consonance and assonance rhymes.

The TV is flashing
potatoes are mashing
as she clears the plates off the table
and sighs at the dishes
and silently wishes
she'll find a way out when she's able

The section is still AABCCB, but the degree of closure is extremely strong in lines 1 and 2 and lines 4 and 5. Similarly, the connections between the third line "table" and the closing line "able" are equally hard to ignore. What happened to our content when we limited our options to perfect rhyme? In this case, the content of line 2 depended on the available rhymes "stashing, smashing, cashing, hashing, bashing," etc. The possibilities were even smaller when we considered perfect rhymes for "table." What results is a lyric that settles for less than the original meaning we intend. Rather than prevent myself from ever using the word "table" in a song again, I can look outside the obvious rhymes. That way, I'm never a foregone conclusion in the ears of a critical audience. There is a strong possibility here that the perfect rhymes drew attention because of their obvious quality. So there are sometimes two common problems associated with perfect rhyme:

1. Limited content
2. Strong finality that draws attention

Each case is different, but our ears will often let us know if the rhyme is taking us down one of those two dead-end roads. Now, let's see what happens when we don't rhyme at all. The content is completely unpredictable with no closure at any point during the section:

The TV is flashing
And blurred in the hallway
As she clears the plates off the table
And sighs at the dishes
And slips out a postcard
Hid in the can with the coffee

Especially now that we're familiar with where to expect the rhymes, the whole section sounds awkward. At no place do we hear any common thread between the lines. We could conclude then that rhyme strengthens the sense that certain content and words "belong" in the song.

There is another important conclusion as to the structure of rhyme and how it relates to music. In the next chapter, we'll explore how this relationship makes it possible to write lyrics before writing the music and still arrive at a song that achieves all our musical goals.

Now that we've gotten a little background on rhyme, let's gather those tools to help us maximize the musical setting of our lyrics.

Chapter Summary

1. Rhyme pairs can be created from both the middle and the end of external and internal phrases.
2. The five types of rhyme from strongest degree of closure to least are perfect, family, additive/subtractive, assonance, and consonance.
3. The position the rhyme holds in the line and the position the rhyme holds in the section determine the amount of closure the rhyme pair provides.
4. Common problems associated with rhyme are limited content and strong finality that draws attention.
5. Both strict and loose rhyme can result in a loss of connection.
6. Our most valuable asset is our ears.

CHAPTER 5

Reflections of Music Form and Structure

THE LANGUAGE OF PHRASING

As writers, we may fancy ourselves poets or storytellers. But as lyricists, we've got to keep a strong hold on those reins of free-flowing prose. Connecting with our listener requires signals, keying them in to when sections begin and when they end and which phrases are most central to the main point and which are not.

Imagine that lyrics are like the map of a theme park. Now imagine the music was the actual theme park itself. As you walk past the cotton candy kiosk, around the giant teacup ride and over the walking bridge to the Tilt-a-Whirl, you follow each point on your map. But when you finally arrive at the rickety, ex-con–operated thrill ride, you realize that your map actually shows a food court in its place. Thinking that you've misread the map, you spend the next moments trying to coordinate yourself with other landmarks. Everything else checks out, but you can't shake the feeling you're not where the map says you're supposed to be.

The same goes for the relationship between music and lyrics. Just as a lyric has structure that is made up of lines, music has structure that is made up of phrases. The signals of structure and rhyme that are present in a lyric must coincide with the signals of structure and rhyme in the music. Even before we compose the music, we can get an idea of what the music will look like because of the lyric structure and rhyme scheme we choose.

So what are the signals of structure and rhyme? And why is it important to heed the signals and follow their direction?

To answer these questions, we must first be able to hear a musical phrase. Song melodies aren't just meandering notes scattered across an unpredictable number of bars. They are large ideas made up of smaller ideas called "phrases." These phrases aren't an unpredictable string of notes either, but are related in rhythm and interval. The rhythms and intervals throughout the melody and harmony repeat over and over, giving the song a consistent identity all its own.

Consider "Mary Had a Little Lamb." Let's use the basic rhythm of that nursery rhyme as an example of a four-line section. Feel the matching rhythms of lines 1 and 3 and lines 2 and 4, as you read along:

Mary had a little lamb
whose fleece was white as snow
and everywhere that Mary went
the lamb was sure to go

There are four phrases that make up the larger section. Each phrase is a group of notes that provide one valuable link in the whole tune's entity. Again, we might think of a phrase in terms of a roadmap. Let's say you want to travel from Pittsburgh to New York City, so you plot your course along Highway 70. And along the way, you plan on stopping several times, just to make sure you're still on course. The distance from Pittsburgh to your first stop is one musical phrase, or in our nursery rhyme, "Mary had a little lamb." The distance from your first stop to your second stop is another phrase, line 2 in our four-line scheme. The second stop to the third stop is another phrase, line 3, and finally the third stop to the Big Apple is the final phrase of the trip, line 4. Now, you may be thinking that this is utterly elementary and considering skipping ahead to the next few pages. But in my experience, there is no greater misunderstanding of young and old writers alike than the way we notate our lyrical phrases on paper. Each line denotes a musical phrase. Each musical phrase denotes a lyrical line. They must coincide for the lyric to ultimately be applicable to a melody and harmony in a way that makes musical sense.

Let's take our roadmap analogy one step further. Say you decide to stop at a sketchy little gas station between Pittsburgh and your first stop. Because it's not a major city, you find yourself feeling lost, pulled over in an area where there really aren't any signs that you're still on the right path. So wisely, you get back in your car and drive the rest of the way to your first scheduled stop to fill up. Put in musical terms, stopping before you get to the end of a phrase will also leave your listener lost, searching for signs that they're still on the right path. Let's look at this in another way. Stopping in the middle of a musical phrase would be as if you paused mid-sentence while having a conversation. Your listeners would likely wonder if there was some emphasis, some greater point that unfortunately they missed. Undoubtedly, they would intuitively know that something was wrong. The result would be a few strange looks and a guarantee that whatever you were talking about would be overshadowed by the way you were talking about it.

Because of the rhythm of the nursery rhyme, we know the phrasing is four lines. Let's denote one phrase as an arrow, pointing us all the way to the end of the line before stopping and starting again.

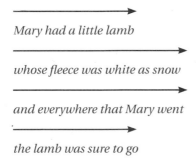

Mary had a little lamb

whose fleece was white as snow

and everywhere that Mary went

the lamb was sure to go

So far, we've talked about phrases as lengths of lines. But we can also talk about phrasing in terms of rhyme scheme. The verse above has a rhyme scheme of ABAB. What does the rhyme scheme have to do with phrasing? Like we did in our previous chapter on rhyme, let's replace the existing scheme with a different one to hear how rhyme affects the overall phrasing of the tune.

Mary had a little horse
Whose hair was dark as night
And everywhere that Mary went
The horse would follow too

The length of the lines has remained the same, so we know it is not an issue of rhythm that is throwing us off. When we change the rhyme scheme, something interesting happens. That last line suddenly feels awkward, as if it doesn't belong. The reason is that the musical phrasing signals the presence of a rhyme scheme that does not actually come to pass. The musical phrasing is giving us road signs, but when we finally arrive at our destination, the promises those signs make aren't fulfilled. This leads us to an important conclusion about the relationship between rhyme and musical phrasing:

> Rhyme reflects the length of a musical phrase.
> A musical phrase suggests the placement of rhyme.

FOUR-LINE SECTIONS

Musical phrases are markers that suggest where rhymes fall. In a four-line section, there are three typical schemes used over and over again in popular song. They are:

1. XAXA
2. ABAB
3. AABB

When these rhyme schemes are not occurring, something must be occurring musically to accommodate. For example, the last line may be broken into two shorter phrases that rhyme with each other:

Mary had a little horse
whose hair was dark as night
and everywhere that Mary went
the horse would go
with eyes aglow

This scheme would be written as XAXBB, but is sometimes mistaken for XAXA. It is important to note that the rhyme between "go" and "aglow" is what breaks the line in two. Rhythmically, those two phrases together equal a slightly longer phrase than one of the previous lines. The line could also be extended where only one rhyme occurs, but still later than expected:

Mary had a little horse
whose hair was dark as night
and everywhere that Mary went
the horse would gladly let young Mary ride

This scheme is still XAXA, but the last line is lengthened to reflect a lengthening in the musical phrasing. In both of these verses, the placement of the rhyme reflects the length of each musical phrase.

In the last two examples, the nursery rhyme has encountered a lengthening of the last line. Let's look at another variation of the scheme XAXA in which the last line is shortened.

Mary had a little horse
whose hair was dark as night
and everywhere that Mary went
he'd hide

Now the rhyme occurs sooner than we expect, the musical phrasing closing with the rhyme "hide." Here again, the musical phrasing suggests the early placement of the rhyme, and the rhyme reflects the early close of the musical phrase.

We can summarize the possibilities for four-line sections of XAXA, ABAB, and AABB as follows:

1. Shortened and doubled last line
2. Lengthened last line
3. Shortened last line

By viewing sections as alterations of a four-line structure, we can more easily make sense of what is occurring.

SIX-LINE SECTIONS

Let's look at another common structure to better understand the relationship between lyric and music. This structure used in popular songs over and over again is six-lines, often occurring with the following rhyme scheme:

("T" represents the title line appearing in the section.)

1. XXAXXA
2. AABCCB
3. ABCABC
4. XXTXXT
5. AATBBT
6. ABTABT

Notice that number 1 and number 4 are similar with the substitution of a title line. The same goes for numbers 2/5 and 3/6.

Just like the four-line section, the six-line section is made up of two halves. Each half is a three-line group followed by another three-line group. In the song "That's Amore," there are two groups of three lines making up the six-line section. This section has a rhyme scheme of AATBBT, the title appearing in the middle and last line of the lyric.

"That's Amore" by Jack Brooks and Harry Warren

When the moon hits your eye	A
like a big pizza pie	A
that's amore	T
When the world seems to shine	B
like you've had too much wine	B
that's amore	T

At first glance it looks and sounds like a simple six-line verse. But let's see what happens when we change the rhyme scheme, shortening the phrases by providing rhyme halfway through each line:

If you jump	A
if you spin	B
if you run	A
if you grin	B
that's amore	T

Now this half of the original verse looks like a four-line section plus a title line. Often, the section that is written as ABABT can also be written as AAT. The difference is the length of the musical phrases we choose to reflect with our lyrical phrases.

When we write our own lyric, it is only important that we identify which structure we're working towards: four-line or six-line with some alteration of either a shortened or lengthened line. That way, we'll always know that what we're accomplishing lyrically can easily be represented musically. For example, I'll rewrite the first half of the verse in order to reflect the same phrasing patterns as my rewrite:

When the moon
hits your eye
like a big
pizza pie
that's amore

If you jump
if you spin
if you run
if you grin
that's amore

Having the ability to distill each section of your song to a simpler structure will help to identify and fix problem areas. Even the most complex melodies have identifiable patterns and some degree of predictability that is pleasant to our ears.

EXERCISE 5.1. Creating Four- and Six-Line Sections

Practice combining the lines below into either four- or six-line sections. You may have to add, subtract, and reorder the lines in order to fulfill the rhyme scheme.

Line 1: Where sound disappears   Line 4: Way up above all the static

Line 2: The lights, noise, and traffic   Line 5: Dust caught in sunbeams

Line 3: Higher than thunder and jet streams   Line 6: And thin atmospheres

Four-Line Possibility 1

A _____

B _____

A _____

B _____

Four-Line Possibility 2

A _____

B _____

C _____

B _____

Six-Line Possibility 1

A _____

A _____

B _____

C _____

C _____

B _____

Six-Line Possibility 2

A _____

B _____

C _____

A _____

B _____

C _____

PHRASING AND CONTENT

We now understand how lyrical phrases represent musical phrases and vice versa. But there is another subtler relationship between the marriage of music and lyric. So far, we've been talking about structure and rhyme scheme—the architectural plans of our lyric. Now we're going to talk about the building itself in all its spires and awnings. In this correlation, we're going to apply what we know about phrasing to the progression of content within the lyric.

The closing of a large rhyme scheme often signals the closure of a lyrical topic. Similarly, the closure of a larger musical phrase often signals the end of a larger lyrical topic.

Let's go back to Mary and her little lamb. Earlier we talked about the four-line verse being made up of four equally long phrases. But when we talk about content, we're going to look at the bigger picture with the composite of smaller phrases into larger phrases. The nursery rhyme can be described as two large phrases, each one line long. These phrases cannot be combined any further to achieve an even larger phrase because the melody at the end of each line resolves and repeats. They are the largest representation of the phrasing of Mary and her lamb:

> *Mary had a little lamb whose fleece was white as snow*
> *And everywhere that Mary went the lamb was sure to go*

Now if you'll entertain me for a moment, let's analyze the content of these two lines. The first thing we notice is that each large phrase is one sentence or complete phrase, not a fragment of a sentence or phrase. That alone is a lyrical clue suggesting these two lines are the largest possible phrases. We also notice that at the close of the first large phrase, the content progresses to another topic rather than continuing the initial focus. Let me illustrate what would happen if the content of line 1 were continued through line 2:

> *Mary had a little lamb whose fleece was white as snow*
> *With hooves black and polished clean and eyes blue and bold*

By continuing the content of the first line, we are creating a section that is written about one "topic." Both variations, either one topic or two, may serve our overall message of the song.

Now let's see what happens when the content changes topic before the phrasing closes.

Mary had a little lamb whose fleece was white and home

was where the two would always stay when rain would fall in droves

Just as we established in previous pages that musical phrases represent the length of lyrical phrases, the same applies to content. A musical phrase is like a sentence. Starting a new topic mid-sentence will draw attention to how you're speaking rather than what you're speaking about. Your listener will either look at you with confusion and ask you to repeat what you just said, or kindly but quickly excuse herself from the conversation.

The effect of closing a lyrical phrase down before the musical phrase closes down is even more awkward at the end of a section. In the rewrite below, we're left with a sentence fragment that requires us to hold on until the new section begins:

Mary had a little lamb whose fleece was white as snow

and everywhere that Mary went he'd go and Mary found

Someone good at tending him and walking him at home

so she could get some sleeping in and finally be alone

At the conclusion of the first verse, we're left pausing on "found," asking "found what?" The broken phrase takes our focus off of the meaning of the lyric and onto how awkward it's being said. Instead, we'd do better to find another way of saying the same thing while keeping to the phrasing set by the melody:

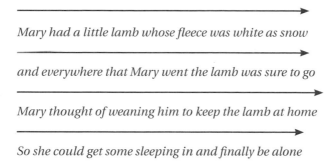

Mary had a little lamb whose fleece was white as snow

and everywhere that Mary went the lamb was sure to go

Mary thought of weaning him to keep the lamb at home

So she could get some sleeping in and finally be alone

Now let's experiment with changing the content midway through each larger phrase, adhering to the signals of closure the smaller phrases provide. In other words, let's try combining four separate content ideas for each of the four smaller phrases:

Mary had a little lamb and Mary had a pony too

the sun was rising in the east and May was slipping into June

Each line introduces a new thought. And just as we begin to picture the new thought, we are quickly ushered onto the next. The result of using smaller musical phrases to dictate topic movement is jerky, surface-oriented content. As you can see, the more topics that are introduced, the less the time that can be given to convincing detail. As artists, we're trying to create a connection with our listener. Our goal must be to identify the experience we're trying to cause. If it is an experience of light-hearted fun, skimming the surface may be appropriate for causing that experience. But if we are aiming for authentic, deep-felt emotion, then surface detail just won't do.

The chart below outlines the number of topics typically introduced in a section of four or six lines. Like our typical rhyme schemes suggest in the beginning of this chapter, these sections are commonly made up of two equal halves. In a four-line section, we typically have two choices for content:

1. All four lines continue one idea.
2. Two lines of one idea are followed by two lines of another idea.

LISTENING SUGGESTIONS FOR FOUR-LINE SECTIONS
Marc Cohn, "Walking in Memphis"
Nickelback, "Someday, Somehow"
Don Henley, "Boys of Summer"

In a six-line section, some common choices are:

1. All six lines continue one idea.
2. Three lines of one idea are followed by three lines of another idea.

LISTENING SUGGESTIONS FOR SIX-LINE SECTIONS
Avril Lavigne, "I'm with You"
Faith Hill, "You Stay with Me"
Mark Wills, "Don't Laugh at Me"

Number of Lines	Rhyme Scheme	Number of Topics
2	XX AA	1–2
4	XAXA ABAB AABB	1–2
6	XXAXXA AABCCB ABCABC	1–2

You might see a pattern emerging here. Even if the section is an odd number of lines, the content consists of either one or two topics, with the added line continuing the topic introduced with the second half of the section. You may find this chart summarizing some typical structures, rhyme schemes, and topic movements helpful as a reference when constructing your next song.

Chapter Summary

1. Just as lyrics have structure that is made up of lines, music has structure that is made up of phrases.
2. Rhyme scheme reflects the length of musical phrases.
3. Musical phrases suggest the placement of rhyme.
4. Two very common verse structures are four and six lines.
5. The closing of a large musical phrase suggests the closing of a large lyrical idea.

CHAPTER 6

Writing the Verse

SECRETS OF STRUCTURE

Up until this point, we've talked about rhyme, phrasing, and content. We've even learned to distinguish external phrases from internal phrases and how to identify and combine naturally occurring rhymes into paired ideas. Throughout these chapters, I hope you've been exercising your destination-writing muscles, using the where, who, and when lists from appendix A as your keywords.

Now, we're going to get to the heart of the songwriting process. I have found it helpful to break down the process of songwriting into ten steps. You're already familiar with the first two steps, destination writing/creating columns and finding rhyme pairs, as well as the importance verbs play in the overall strength of the experience.

Step 1. **Destination-write and create columns**
Step 2. **Find rhyme pairs**
Step 3. Choose a rhyme scheme and toggling pattern
Step 4. Add prepositions and conjunctions
Step 5. Choose a plot progression
Step 6. Destination-write again using thought/feeling language
Step 7. Look for titles and write the chorus
Step 8. Write a second verse and prechorus
Step 9. Write the bridge
Step 10. **Verbs**, tense, point of view, and conversational quality

Now we're going to apply steps 3 and 4, combining our internal and external rhyme pairs to create song sections we never would have come up with otherwise.

We know that song lyrics follow patterns of rhythm, rhyme, and content. These patterns appear over and over again in all different styles of music. We also know we can use these patterns as models for our own songs. But this next pattern I'm going to propose to you results in a tool for developing content rather than structure. It is a process I call "toggling." Toggling is a strategy for organizing song content. It is a means of combining external and internal detail to arrive at a skillfully written section.

There are many different toggling patterns, but rhyme scheme and number of lines in a particular section offer great clues as to which pattern to use. Crafting our song sections with toggling helps us achieve a few important results:

- A properly weighted section
- Contrast between sections
- A more intense experience
- Presentation of our best ideas

Let's visualize the process of toggling by looking at the first verse of the song "Why Georgia" by John Mayer.

"Why Georgia"

I am driving up 85
in the kind of morning that lasts all afternoon
just stuck inside the gloom
Four more exits to my apartment
but I am tempted to keep the car in drive
and leave it all behind

You might have already analyzed this verse as having six lines and a rhyme scheme of XAAXBB. If you didn't notice, cut yourself a break. This is a learning process, and you'll get the hang of it the more you actively try to look for these characteristics. Now, what about content? Are there patterns within the content of the lines that yield clues to how we could write our own verse?

The answer, as you may now suspect, is yes, there certainly is. We already discussed one clue in the previous chapter: a section being made up of one or even two topics, changing midway through the section as the rhyme scheme repeats. In this verse, the content reflects that pattern with each three-line group making up a complete sentence or thought. But there is another even more useful pattern present within this section. It has to do with the movement between external and internal detail. In many songs, this movement can feel a bit like "toggling" between the two types of detail. To identify the toggling pattern, we first need to identify the function of each line as either internal or external detail. Let's return to those discerning questions from chapter 3:

> Does the phrase describe what's going on around the main character?

If so, then the detail is external.

> Does the phrase describe what's going on within the heart or mind of the main character?

If so, then the detail is internal.

Now, going back to this verse, let's assign each line an identity: external or internal, or in some cases, both.

"Why Georgia" by John Mayer

I am driving up 85	External
in the kind of morning that lasts all afternoon	External/Internal
just stuck inside the gloom	Internal
Four more exits to my apartment	External
but I am tempted to keep the car in drive	External/Internal
and leave it all behind	Internal

We can see here that lines 2 and 5 have both external and internal qualities. In line 2, the idea of a morning lasting all afternoon is more abstract and metaphorical than a morning that lasts until 11:59 A.M. That quality shifts the detail from concrete external to slightly more internal and abstract. Similarly, line 5 shifts the external detail of keeping the car in drive to slightly internal when the feeling of being tempted comes into play.

This multiple identity is typical of lines later in a song. As a song progresses, the lines often become more internal and abstract. The stronger the foundation of concrete detail we have to build on, the more abstract internal detail can add dimension later on in the song. It's all a matter of value. Without a particular image to give value to, the internal detail fails to cause an experience.

A good way to find out if a line is more external or internal is to try switching out the line in question for a purely external or purely internal detail. If the section feels heavy and cluttered, a more abstract line will alleviate the problem. But if the section becomes weak and flimsy, then a more concrete line is needed. We can then make educated decisions on how to combine the external and internal characteristics to arrive at a section with the proper weight, keeping the focus centered on the content and not on how we're presenting it.

Now that we've got a pretty good handle on the type of detail of each line, we can take a look at the overall pattern. What do you notice about the order of external and internal detail? They create a pattern that establishes itself in the first half of the verse, and repeats in the second half. That pattern is External External/ Internal Internal, External External/Internal Internal. At the position the musical phrases begin and close, the toggling pattern also begins and closes. What emerges is a roadmap for content that we can apply to our own song sections.

The toggling structure for this verse is written as E E/I I E E/I I, a very effective pattern for six-line verses. To understand why this pattern is so popular, let's try changing it. What do you think will happen to the flow of content? Or better yet, how will it affect the experience and connection we cause our listener? Let's experiment with this idea by first replacing the last three external details with internal details.

> *I am driving up 85*
> *in the kind of morning that lasts all afternoon*
> *just stuck inside the gloom*
> *I've been thinking how sadness comes around*
> *every time that my hopes get up too soon*
> *and there's nothing I can do*

It's not bad, but we lose some valuable information. With internal detail, we are in effect "telling" our audience how the subject feels instead of creating an experience of that feeling. The first two lines create a good deal of imagery that sustains through the second half, but I wonder if the abstract nature of lines 3 and 4 compromise the ability of the verse to create an experience. The experience itself will always be more powerful than the relation of that experience. Now, let's try the opposite approach, this time loading the last three lines to the brim with external detail. You may also think about "weight" when you read and experience this section:

> *I am driving up 85*
> *in the kind of morning that lasts all afternoon*
> *just stuck inside the gloom*
> *Four more exits to my apartment*
> *and white lines dotting a distant stretch of road*
> *with trees hanging low*

Now the effect is dramatic. Instead of keeping an intimate connection with the listener, the song continues with external detail that fails to relate back to the subject. We're left with a heaviness in that last line, wondering what "trees hanging low" has to do with the main point of the song.

Let's try one more variation on this toggle pattern, this time placing the internal detail right up front in the first three lines:

> *I've been thinking how sadness comes around*
> *every time that my hopes get up too soon*
> *and there's nothing I can do*
> *I've been driving up 85*
> *in the kind of morning that lasts all afternoon*
> *just stuck inside the gloom*

The external details that so beautifully captured the experience in the original first three lines are delayed until halfway through the verse. The thoughts and feelings that now begin the verse can't color the external detail we haven't yet heard, and so are difficult to relate to. I like to compare this type of result to salting a steak after you've eaten it. Salting an empty plate after that last bite of cow doesn't do anything to make the T-bone in your stomach taste better. It's the same with external and internal detail. External detail presented early on will color the experience of the internal detail to follow. Internal detail can't make the experience of external detail to follow more authentic, no matter how true our intentions may be.

Internal detail does a wonderful job of bringing purpose to detail. After we've described an image, we can give that image a point in the song by commenting about how we feel or think about that image. John Mayer does this with "just stuck inside the gloom" and "and leave it all behind." This brings up an interesting point regarding the last line of a section, sitting in a position called the "power position." Frequently, this power position receives its influence from its ability, or rather responsibility, to sum up the meaning of the whole section. Just by shifting the content of this last line from external detail to internal thoughts and feelings, we can sum up the song and bring closure to the ideas presented.

Many toggling patterns end with an internal detail, regardless of the initial half of the verse pattern repeating itself. Without the culmination of the content summed up in that last line, the content has no purpose.

We can think of summarizing a section with internal detail in another way. Imagine I was telling you how this morning I rose around 5 A.M., thumbed a cab ride to the airport, and sweated in my overcoat, as I ran through the crowded sidewalks dragging my two overstuffed suitcases and bulky carry-on behind me, then blew into the ticket counter before racing down the halls to security. You'd look at me with an expression of "then what?" Or maybe even "why are you telling me this?" Our audience is no different. They desire a point to our stories, too.

There are different toggling patterns that prove to be effective for different rhyme schemes, but much of their effectiveness depends on our ability to "feel" or "sense" the proper weight of the section. Sometimes, the toggling pattern is repeated halfway through a section. Sometimes the pattern lasts throughout the section. We merely need to open our ears and eyes and become aware of the patterns we see working in other songs. Then if in our own song we feel we could strengthen the experience by substituting an external detail for an internal one or vice versa, we can. But these basic toggling patterns can be life changing for a songwriter, giving us a springboard from which to organize our ideas and achieve the greatest flexibility with those ideas.

Below is a chart of common toggling patterns and their typical rhyme scheme partners often found in hit songs. The more fluent you become with the patterns and schemes listed here, the greater success and flexibility you will find in altering these patterns.

Number of Lines	Toggle Pattern	Rhyme Scheme
2	EI II	XX AA
4	EEEI EIEI IEII	XAXA ABAB AABB
6	EEIEEI EIEEII IEIIEI	XXAXXA AABCCB ABCABC

Once in a while, beginning with internal detail can suffice in grabbing the attention of our audience. The verse below begins with internal detail, saving the external for later:

Her love was a Tilt-a-Whirl
spinning me around
she had me running circles
till the day she tossed me out

It's not until lines 3 and 4 that we get some concrete detail; however, the word "Tilt-a-Whirl" carries some weight as an image. Many songs that use immediate internal detail employ a metaphor. Here, that metaphor is a theme park ride, continuing throughout the verse and later through the whole song. Metaphor alone is sometimes strong enough to give the song a flavor that creates a lasting impression. It's also a great way to stay away from generalities when we write. This same verse without the use of metaphor could easily fall into Never-Never Land, bland and lacking connection:

Her love was capricious
spinning me around
she had me running circles
till the day she tossed me out

The greatest power of a metaphor is often its ability to paint a picture in our minds. When we present that picture early on in the song and build on it, we keep adding dimension and connection to the song. Shifting from metaphor to metaphor within the same song can inhibit connection by keeping the listener on the surface of many ideas instead of deeply rooted in a single idea.

EXERCISE 6.1. Toggling In Action

Practice toggling the lines below into two-, four-, and six-line sections using the following toggling patterns: EEII, EIEI, IIEE, and EIEEIE.

I brushed away the cobwebs	E
and dusted 'round the door	E
as musty memories filled my mind	I
I pulled back the curtains	E
and let sunlight flood the floor	E
and all that slept within me sighed	I

Possible Answers:

I brushed away the cobwebs	E
and dusted 'round the door	E
as musty memories filled my mind	I
all that slept within me sighed	I

I brushed away the cobwebs	E
as musty memories filled my mind	I
I pulled back the curtains	E
and all that slept within me sighed	I

Musty memories filled my mind	I
all that slept within me sighed	I
and as I dusted 'round the door	E
I let the sunlight flood the floor	E

I brushed away the cobwebs	E
as musty memories filled my mind	I
and dusted 'round the door	E
I pulled back the curtains	E
and all that slept within me sighed	I
I let sunlight flood the floor	E

Which of these verses feels most natural and, in your estimation, produces the strongest experience?

EXERCISE 6.2. Applied Toggling

Write an original verse from any of your daily destination writings. Using your external and internal columns, toggle either a four- or six-line section using the rhyme-scheme and pattern possibilities listed in the toggling chart.

FILLING IN MISSING LINES

Sometimes, when we're toggling, we find we're missing an external or internal detail to complete the rhyme scheme. If our destination writing has not supplied us with all the rhymes or content we need, we simply plug in the phrases we do have and then write a new line. As long as we follow the toggling pattern with our new line, the idea will work no matter what it is.

Let's assume we've got three lines of a four-line section and wish to write a fourth thought/feeling line (an internal detail). So far, the section looks like this:

	Toggling Pattern	Rhyme Scheme
There were trash cans by driveways	External	X
and lawn chairs in the snow	External	A
as I drove past the houses	External	X
?	Internal	A

It doesn't matter what detail we write for that last line, as long as it deals with the thoughts and feelings of the character. It should be abstract as opposed to concrete:

	Toggling Pattern	Rhyme Scheme
There were trash cans by driveways	External	X
and lawn chairs in the snow	External	A
as I drove past the houses	External	X
I felt so alone	Internal	A

I could easily insert a completely different thought/feeling detail:

	Toggling Pattern	Rhyme Scheme
There were trash cans by driveways	External	X
and lawn chairs in the snow	External	A
as I drove past the houses	External	X
I thought I'd outgrown	Internal	A

The same is true for the external lines. Any concrete detail can be replaced with any other concrete detail:

	Toggling Pattern	Rhyme Scheme
There were trash cans by driveways	External	X
and squares on the lawns	External	A
where light spilled from windows	External	X
and my memories were drawn	Internal	A

All we need to do is make sure we're choosing our rhymes effectively, matching the level of originality of the rest of our destination-writing-inspired section.

CONNECTING A TOGGLED SECTION

Gaining the ability to combine our phrase fragments into effective sections is a huge step. But now, we're going to learn how to connect those phrases so they no longer seem like separate pieces of a larger puzzle. The secret to connection lies in tiny words called prepositions and conjunctions (for a list, refer to appendix B). After we've inserted the phrases from our columns into our rhyme scheme and toggle pattern, we can add prepositions and conjunctions wherever needed to make complete sentences. The ability of our section to create an experience will depend on our ability to make the section as conversational as possible. The more conversational and natural the section sings, the stronger the connection our audience will feel.

Let's use the section below, taken from my columns on "Airport." Each line feels like a separate fragmented detail when plugged into the toggling pattern and rhyme scheme:

Chair exhaled, I slumped down	External	X
A barbell, at the gate	External	A
Combed my fingers through my hair	External	X
Give in to the wait (new line)	Internal	A

When the connector words are added (indicated in bold), the verse takes on life:

The chair exhaled as I slumped down	External	X
like a barbell at the gate	External	A
and combed my fingers through my hair	External	X
and gave in to the wait	Internal	A

Simply adding words like "the, like, as, and, but, with, while," and pronouns like "I," we can turn a stack of phrases into a conversational section. Notice that the verse adheres to our ideas on phrasing. In this case, the whole section is one topic simply because of the word "and." Conjunctions and prepositions have the power to either insert a pause or keep the sentence going. Here, I've divided the section into two halves, each half a complete thought on its own:

The chair exhaled as I slumped down	External	X
like a barbell at the gate	External	A
I combed my fingers through my hair	External	X
and gave in to the wait	Internal	A

Sometimes the effects of conjunctions and prepositions are dramatic enough to create a feeling of stopping and starting within a section. If those stops and starts don't correspond with the beginnings and endings of the musical phrasing, we run into Mary and her little lamb's problem again. The good thing is it's often simple to reconnect phrases to match our musical phrasing.

Let's look at another example of how adding prepositions and conjunctions turns a fragmented stack of details into a singable section. This time, let's use Aunt Louise from chapter 2 as our subject. I've drawn external and internal details from my destination writing to construct the sections below:

Verse 1:
Drew the tattered washcloth
Pan with grease
Wisps of hair fell in her eyes
Brushed them behind her ears

Verse 2:
Cleared the dishes from the table
Hear her humming
things weren't great at my own home
place I belonged

Here I've constructed two four-line verse ideas with a loose rhyme scheme XAXA. The first verse follows a toggling pattern of EEEE, then the second verse changes the last two lines to internal. Because of the heavy external detail throughout the first and second verse, those last few lines are extremely important in giving both sections value. As it reads now, there seems to be a strong disconnect between the ideas. But when I add in some tiny connectors, the story begins to emerge:

Verse 1:

She drew the tattered washcloth
over the pan with grease
as wisps of hair fell in her eyes
and she brushed them behind her ears

Verse 2:

And as I cleared the dishes from the table
I listened to her hum
Even though this wasn't my real home
she made me feel that I belonged

In the second line of verse 2, I wanted to accentuate the sound of "-um" and "-ong" to really grab that loose rhyme. That meant I had to change the tense of the verb "humming." I kept the idea for the content of that line, but rearranged the wording to achieve the rhythm and rhyme. Then I added the pronoun "I" to benefit the conversational quality of the verse.

EXERCISE 6.3. Using Conjunctions and Prepositions

Practice adding conjunctions and prepositions to the four-line sections below. Use the list of prepositions and conjunctions in appendix B for ideas. Experiment with different connectors to hear how they each change the meaning of the content.

standing in the place I started from
room I spent my life escaping from
painted dresser and a single bed
curtains hanging like a high school prom dress

Possible Answer:

I'm standing in the place I started from
in the room I spent my life escaping from
with a painted dresser and a single bed
and curtains hanging like a high school prom dress

THE THREE ELEMENTS

In the pages ahead, we're going to look at another characteristic of great songs. Once you're aware of this tool at work, you can decide how the songs you write would benefit from its application.

An important aspect of content we can learn from our favorite songs is the presence of "who," "where," and "when." In most songs, these three characteristics go unnoticed, just taken for granted as part of the natural flow of the lyric. But the simple omission of just one of these elements can seriously jeopardize our connection with our audience. Let's first look at what we mean when we look for the presence of these three elements.

In the lyric below, we can easily identify who, where, and when:

"Time after Time," by Cyndi Lauper and Robert Hyman

Lying in my bed
I hear the clock tick
and think of you
caught up in circles
confusion
is nothing new

This lyric is written in first person perspective. "Who" is "my/ I." "Where" is "in my bed." "When" is sometimes more difficult to identify, because it is rarely found stated as "six o'clock" or "this morning." Instead, it is reflected in the form of being "lying." Because of the present form of being, the "when" is "right now," or "as the song is being sung."

Sometimes, these three elements are subtler. In the following lyric, "when" is still reflected in the tense of the verbs, but "where" is revealed in the detail as early as line 2, placing us somewhere on a busy sidewalk. We still get "who" right up front in line 1 with the pronoun "I."

Who   When   Where

I pull my coat in tight
and drift through the morning sidewalk crowds
slip by the newsstand lines
and breathe in the grease and coffee grounds
here in the stream of traffic
I see the years that pass me by
each one drives hard and fast and
I might still be asking why

No matter how subtle the presence of these elements, they clearly give the listener a time, a place, and a subject early on in the song. Think of these three elements as legs of a tripod. If any one of them is missing, the song loses its footing and the audience feels it. No matter how hard we try to convince our audience that they should understand where we're coming from, they won't quite buy it. Let's see what happens when we omit the presence of these elements:

I pulled my coat in tight
And drift through the confusion
Slipping by the printed lines
And breathe in the illusion

Any one of the lines are just fine on their own, even great in the appropriate context, but as a whole, the experience this lyric causes is confusing. I've made a few minor changes to sabotage this lyric. The first was playing with the tense of the verbs, creating confusion with "when." The first line is about an event that happened, but the second line is a command form of something that is happening. Now that we're not sure whether this event is happening or has happened, we're spending our attention trying to make sense of the detail rather than experiencing the detail. I've also removed a sense of "where" from the lyric. This omission leaves the artist floating out in the world of feelings and thoughts without an image for the listener to grab onto.

Imagine a friend telling you that she just broke up with her boyfriend. Knowing when and where it happened would certainly allow you to connect better with her head and heart, imagining the experience she must have encountered. The more detail you gather about where she was when it happened, the more personal it feels to you. You can give your audience that same personal relationship by cluing them in to where and when your song takes place.

EXERCISE 6.4. Identifying the Three Elements

Identify the three elements in each of the first-verse sections below.

"Why Georgia," by John Mayer

I am driving up 85
in the kind of morning that lasts all afternoon
just stuck inside the gloom
Four more exits to my apartment
but I am tempted to keep the car in drive
and leave it all behind

How is WHO established? _____

How is WHERE established? _____

How is WHEN established? _____

Answers: **Where**: driving up 85   **Who**: I/my   **When**: am, "-ing" of driving

"Breakaway," by Bridget Benenate, Matthew Gerrard, Avril Lavigne

(I) grew up in a small town
and when the rain would fall down
I'd just stare out my window
Dreaming of what could be
and if I'd end up happy
I would pray

How is WHO established? _____

How is WHERE established? _____

How is WHEN established? _____

Answers: **Where**: small town, window   **Who**: I/my   **When**: grew

What do you notice about your answers? Do you find that the three elements most often occur within the first few lines of the song? If you did, then you're on the right track. As with many song-writing techniques, this commonality is a guide but will let us down as a rule.

Let's see what happens when one or more of these elements occur later in the song, perhaps not until the later half of the verse rather than the first half:

> *Her fears had kept her confused in a maze*
> *but her heart was intent on believing he'd change*
> *so she stayed around when most would give up*
> *but the day that she tossed all her clothes in a bag*
> *and spun off with the screech of burnt rubber and pain*
> *was the fifteenth of June but her own Independence Day*

It's not until line 4 that we receive a clear indication of "where" with "clothes in a bag" and "spun off with the screech of burnt rubber," allowing us to imagine first a bedroom of sorts and then a car. "Who" and "when" are still present, but they alone don't seem to convince us to connect. Now, without looking back at this verse you just read—I mean it, don't look—do you remember what those first three lines were about? If you don't, then you're right there with the best of us. Perhaps the most important element in a song is "where." It's an audience's lifeline of connection to an artist. It allows the listeners to experience the event rather than just sit on the sidelines.

EXERCISE 6.5. Applying the Elements

Choose a destination-writing example, and separate your external and internal details into two columns. Toggle a four- and six-line section using your columns, following the rhyme scheme and toggling patterns from this chapter. Then go back and analyze if who, where, and when were established. If any of those elements are missing, go back and put them in by either:

- adding I, you, he, or she
- conforming verbs to the same tense, either past, present, or future
- inserting an external detail to clearly describe "where"

LISTENING SUGGESTIONS

Avril Lavigne, "I'm with You"

Kenny Rogers, "The Gambler"

Faith Hill, "You Stay with Me"

Don Henley, "Boys of Summer"

Michael Jackson, "Thriller"

Tonic, "My Old Man"

Green Day, "Boulevard of Broken Dreams"

Chapter Summary

1. Toggling is a strategy for organizing content by means of combining external and internal detail.

2. Effective toggling patterns create strong experiences in the minds and hearts of the listeners.

3. Any internal detail can be exchanged for another internal detail, and any external detail can be exchanged for another external detail.

4. The more conversational the lyric, the stronger the experience that is caused.

5. A lyric can be made more conversational by the addition of conjunctions and prepositions.

6. The three elements of a strong connection are who, where, and when.

CHAPTER 7

The Chorus

INVENTING "WHY"

So far we've been focusing on "what" to write. Now the time has come when we'll decide on "why." "Why" is the reason we wrote the song. It is the culmination of our detail into one complete solitary thought, producing the "ah-hah" moment we songwriters lust after. A song without a purpose is like a joke without a punch line. And we'd be amazed how often songwriters miss that all-important question, "Why?"

Up until this point, we've focused on detail. We've established that the more sense-bound our writing, the stronger the experience we create for our listener. We know how to combine that detail with prepositions and conjunctions so that the sections connect with our listener. Now we're going to explore steps 6 and 7 of our 10-step process, broadening our focus to the big picture. In fact, that's just what the chorus is: the big picture.

Step 1. **Destination-write and create columns**
Step 2. **Find rhyme pairs**
Step 3. **Choose a rhyme scheme and toggling pattern**
Step 4. **Add prepositions and conjunctions**
Step 5. Choose a plot progression
Step 6. **Destination-write again using thought/feeling language**
Step 7. **Look for titles and write the chorus**
Step 8. Write a second verse and prechorus
Step 9. Write the bridge
Step 10. **Verbs**, tense, point of view, and conversational quality

Imagine again that your verse is like a close-up of a leaf. You describe the veins, the pores, and the chlorophyll. You describe the cool, coarse surface and jagged edges against your fingertips, the fresh green smell, bitter and earthy like juiced wheatgrass at the health-foods counter in the grocery store. Now, you pan out to take in not just the leaf, but the whole tree. And surrounding the tree is a patch of grass atop a small hill. And behind that is the sun slowly sinking in the West. That scene—the one-tree hill and its sunset—is the content of the chorus. Its function is to give every tiny, experiential detail of the song purpose and value.

> The function of the chorus is to give every tiny, experiential detail purpose and value.

TWO TYPES OF CHORUSES

Let's imagine what "why" looks like in terms of two different types of choruses: **abstract/metaphorical** and **list**.

Abstract/metaphorical is the most common type of chorus, consisting of mainly thought and feeling detail that we know as internal, sometimes with a few external details thrown in. Below is an example of this type of chorus.

"Time After Time" by Cyndi Lauper and Robert Hyman

If you're lost you can look
And you will find me
Time after time
If you fall I will catch you
I'll be waiting
Time after time

We don't get a clear sense of "where," and "when" is vague as well. Rather than being rooted in a particular time and place, the detail serves as a broad conclusion to the verse content.

List choruses have quite a different function. They also assign purpose and value to previous external detail, but they do it through snapshots of external detail, like the highlights of the story. The chorus below is an example of a list chorus.

> *We had pipes bursting in the downstairs bath*
> *a leak in the roof and a freeway out back*
> *Friday nights and a bottle of wine was all we could afford*
> *But we had a front porch swing and a setting sun*
> *a handful of hope and two hearts full of love*
> *we were lower than high but higher than some*
> *and we weren't keeping score*
> *back when life was all we were living for*

List choruses provide laundry lists of concrete images, while abstract/metaphorical choruses use feelings, thoughts, and metaphors to drive messages home.

In the pages ahead, we'll spend our time writing abstract/metaphorical choruses. From there, the jump to list choruses depends on more external detail to get the job done. In both cases, the strength of the section most often comes down to the central point, the title.

GREAT TITLES ARE BORN, NOT FOUND

Titles don't often jump out screaming "Pick me, I'm obvious!" Titles can be hard to come by, especially those that are original and specific.

But we don't have to fly blind, hoping to arrive at the bigger picture at just the right moment in the section. We can return to our ten-step strategy and destination-write until the purpose is born.

Destination writing for chorus material is different than destination writing for verses. Instead of sense-bound material, this time we're going to focus on internal detail, those thoughts and feelings. This detail is the meat and potatoes of the chorus, spiked with a few external ideas for seasoning. There are two important considerations when destination writing during the chorus stage. First, we'll need to write from first person point of view, or "I." Writing from another point of view might keep us distanced from our emotions. Second, we need to consider the time frame. Writing as the event is happening will often result in stronger emotions than writing about the event after it has happened.

> Write in first person point of view.
> Write as the event is happening.

The paragraph below is written from the keyword "hotel room." Before I begin destination writing for the chorus, I'll destination-write using the six keys of connection and entertain as many senses as possible. At this point, I'm just gathering ideas and getting into the scene:

KEYWORD: `Hotel Room (Verse)`

```
I swiped my card and waited for the little light
to turn green. The door stuck slightly and exhaled
as I unsealed the vacuum and rolled my luggage
behind me into the room. It smelled musty and old,
even though there was the nauseating scent of lemon
cleaner used to disinfect the bathroom. Nursing
homes have that same smell, mixed with the tang of
perm solution and instant coffee. I thought about
how much I missed you, how this would all be bear-
able if you were here. But you're not. The sour
smell made the hairs in my nose curl, and I felt the
cold rush of air-conditioned air that had undoubt-
edly been cranked on high to dispel the mold in the
carpet and the draperies flecked with the grease
from residents before me cooking their meals. Those
were the same smells I caught rolling down the
hall, breathing in the stale air that hung in the
hallways from lack of ventilation and the owner
refusing to spend money on heating and cooling
these transitional areas….
```

After this first destination writing, we are ready to begin destination writing again, reaching for chorus material. I'll write with mainly thoughts and emotions in mind, remembering to use first-person perspective and continuing as if the event is still happening. I may start out with some description and then slowly ease into internal detail, letting whatever thoughts and emotions I can imagine flow through the end of my pen.

KEYWORD: `Hotel Room (Chorus)`

```
    I slumped down on the bed and glanced at the
alarm clock. I still had five hours before going to
work. I felt so out of place here. I wondered what
you were doing right now, if you were thinking of
me. Maybe you were stuck in traffic or shoveling
the snow from the walkway, checking your watch and
calculating when my flight would get in. Maybe you
were telling someone about me, how we talk about
when this job ends and I don't have to spend most of
my weeks on the road. Sometimes I wonder if that's
what keeps us going. We're always looking ahead to
something, believing it will come but never really
knowing when. I wonder what would happen to us if
it did. If tomorrow I quit would it really be every-
thing I thought it would be? Or would I be let down
knowing that I've just given up the best hope we've
got. Always have to leave something aside, like a
cat leaving a little food. Just in case there comes
a day when there isn't anything else. So we save a
little bit, we hide a little piece of ourselves to
make sure it's gonna be alright.
```

Notice that I didn't prevent images and external details to come out when I thought of them. I just allowed ideas to flow and tried to come back to thoughts and feelings whenever I realized I was getting off track.

Now that I have my second destination writing, the next step is to isolate some phrases that I like. What I'm looking for are phrases that resonate with me—ideas that have the ability, if ever so slight, to stand alone in the limelight of the title line.

Below I've listed the phrases that catch my ears and eyes.

You're not	Sometimes I wonder
Stuck in traffic	When this job ends
Looking ahead to something	If it did
What keeps us	How we talk
Believing it will come	Never really knowing
Everything I thought	The best hope we've got
Leave something	Save a little bit
Hide a little piece	

Sometimes, unlikely phrases turn out to be great titles. Sometimes, they don't. Unearthing original ideas through destination writing will always yield some great lines we never would have come across, titles or not.

So we've got some phrases for a title, but we're still staring at a paragraph form of ideas and hoping to build a chorus out of it. The next step is to organize my phrases into two columns, external and internal, just as we did with our first destination writing to organize verse material. I might create two completely new columns, or I might just add the new material onto the old columns to arrive at even more rhyme possibilities and toggling options.

External

		Internal
swiped my card	sour smell	how much I missed you
little light	hair in my nose curl	this would all be bearable
turn green	cold rush	you're not
door stuck slightly	air-conditioned air	sometimes I wonder
exhaled	cranked on high	stuck in traffic
unsealed the vacuum	dispel the mold	looking ahead to some-
rolled my luggage	carpet	thing
room	draperies flecked	what keeps us
musty and old	grease	believing it will come
nauseating scent	residents	everything I thought
lemon cleanser	cooking	leave something
disinfect	stale air	hide a little piece
bathroom	hallways	when this job ends
nursing homes	lack of ventilation	if it did
tang of perm solution	owner refusing	how we talk
instant coffee	spend money	never really knowing
healing and cooling		the best hope we've got
		save a little bit

From these two expanded columns, we can see that some rhyme pairs might be end, ahead; thought, not, talk; bit, did; piece, leave. And those are just within the new internal phrase ideas. As more pairs emerge, more ideas for the direction of content will emerge also.

POWERFUL POSITIONS

Before we begin toggling a chorus, we need to decide where to place the title. The title is the punch line. It's the reason we wrote the song. In every chorus, there are strong placement positions for that attention-grabbing phrase. The placement of the title can mean the difference between an audience that stays with us for the second verse and an audience that flips to the oldies channel instead. In chapter 4, we talked about the last line of a verse section that gives the external detail value. That line is often a thought or feeling line. It is the same with choruses. The line is a powerful statement built around strong metaphors or intense feelings that get right to the heart of the matter. But their value is only worth what their verse and prechorus are able to award them. Alone, they carry very weak arguments.

The chorus section typically offers three positions that are perfect for that one-in-a-million moment. They are at the back, the front, and sometimes the middle of the chorus. Just as the power position in other song sections is the closing line of the section, the last line of the chorus almost always gets the limelight:

power position ⟶   *We had pipes bursting in the downstairs*
       bath
       a leak in the roof and a freeway out back
       Friday nights and a bottle of wine was all
       we could afford
       But we had a front porch swing and a
       setting sun
       a handful of hope and two hearts full of
       love
       we were lower than high but higher than
       some
       and we weren't keeping score
power position ⟶   *back when life was all we were living for*

Some choruses have an additional title line halfway through the chorus:

"Love Can Build a Bridge"
by J. Jarvis, Naomi Judd, Paul Overstreet

power position ⟶ *Love can build a bridge*
Between your heart and mine
power position ⟶ *Love can build a bridge*
Don't you think it's time
Don't you think it's time

But there is another important position in the chorus: the line directly before the power position. Its job is to set up the title. More often than not, that bodyguard to the title will be thought and feeling oriented as well, rather than sense bound and detail oriented. Just like the power position, the purpose of that line is to zoom out to a point where the whole landscape is viewable. In the chorus below, the line directly preceding the title is an abstract thought detail:

Love won't take chances anymore
it leaves an open door
just in case the feeling fades
and love don't have faith anymore
it turns and walks away
doesn't even stay
so what does anybody bother falling for
if love won't take chances anymore?

You'll find that it is very difficult to set up the big picture using the microscopic lens we use for concrete external detail. The revision below changes the line directly before the title to a concrete external detail. The effect is an awkward moment that does very little to support the broad idea of the song.

power position ⟶ *Love won't take chances anymore*
it leaves an open door
just in case the feeling fades
power position ⟶ *and love don't have faith anymore*
it turns and walks away
doesn't even stay
it just gets swept under the carpets of these floors
power position ⟶ *if love won't take chances anymore*

This characteristic of zooming outward for the power positions and their bodyguards is true for list choruses as well as abstract/metaphorical choruses.

Great choruses, like other song sections, don't have to be long or complex. Sometimes, they are as simple as one line repeating four times. Other times, lines taken directly from the second destination-writing come together to create a whole section of thought and feeling phrases. The chorus below is comprised of phrases from my second destination writing, with "Sometimes I Wonder" as my title.

Sometimes I wonder
when I'm stuck in traffic
if this job will ever end
'cuz there's something about
never really knowing
that makes it easier to look ahead
would we make it if it did?
Sometimes I wonder

I chose to sandwich this chorus with the title on the front and back of the section. I could have chosen to place the title at the beginning and middle of the section instead:

Sometimes I wonder
when I'm stuck in traffic
if this job will ever end
And sometimes I wonder
if never really knowing
makes it easier to look ahead

I still feel like the last line is hanging out in nowhere, not strong enough to bring closure to the idea. So I'll repeat the title line to carry the weight of the power position:

Sometimes I wonder
when I'm stuck in traffic
if this job will ever end
And sometimes I wonder
if never really knowing
just makes it easier to look ahead
Sometimes I wonder

I could even arrange a simple four-line chorus with the title repeated in the first three lines:

Sometimes I wonder
sometimes I wonder
sometimes I wonder
if this job will ever end

Or if the last line seems too weak, I can rearrange the title to sit in its place:

Sometimes I wonder
if this job will ever end
sometimes I wonder
yeah sometimes I wonder

Being flexible enough to cut, add, shorten, lengthen, and rearrange lines arms us with everything we need to achieve the lyric and music structure we want. Any and all of these choruses would effectively convey the "why" of a song. They only need to present thoughts and feelings to validate the external details presented in the previous song sections.

TOGGLING A CHORUS SECTION

The same techniques of toggling we applied to verses can be applied to choruses. In fact, the pattern we choose for the chorus will often look a little like the inverse of the verse. (Interesting how that bit of wordplay works out.)

For example, if our verse has a toggling pattern of EEIEEI, our chorus might be IIEIII. (Wherever the title line appears, it is most often more of an internal detail because of its ability to summarize up the broad overview of the song.) The point to remember, when it comes to abstract/metaphorical choruses, is that they are heavier on internal detail than verses. External detail is still useful in giving the internal detail relevance within the chorus. But the difference is that in the chorus section, external detail merely refocuses the abstract detail, returning to those three elements of where, who, and when whenever necessary. Let's see how this idea plays out in the chorus of "Won't Take Chances."

Love won't take chances anymore	I
it leaves an open door	E
just in case the feeling fades	I
and love don't have faith anymore	I
it turns and walks away	E
doesn't even stay	I
so what does anybody bother falling for	I
if love won't take chances anymore	I

Lines 2 and 5 both introduce a concrete image, though used as a metaphor. In the case of line 2, it's an open door, and in the case of line 5, it's the image of turning and walking away. The toggling pattern for the second three-line group is a mirror image of the pattern of the first three-line group. The external detail, though not as literal and concrete as the verse detail, is a great way to spark tiny visuals and keep salting the steak.

Just like verse sections, the toggling pattern for choruses can be viewed as two halves, each a mirror image of the other. The same topic rules that apply to other sections apply to choruses as well.

EXERCISE 7.1. Toggle a Chorus

Practice rearranging the lines below into a four-, five-, and six-line chorus. Try the following toggling patterns: TTIT, ITIT, TITI, IIIT, IIITT, IITIIT.

I can't quite believe
sometimes it's so intense
the way you look at me
it's just a mystery
Love makes no sense

Possible Answers:

TTIT
Love makes no sense
Love makes no sense
it's just a mystery
Love makes no sense

ITIT
The way you look at me
Love makes no sense
I can't quite believe
Love makes no sense

TITI
Love makes no sense
I can't quite believe
Love makes no sense
the way you look at me

IIIT
I can't quite believe
sometimes it's so intense
the way you look at me
Love makes no sense

IIITT
I can't quite believe
sometimes it's so intense
the way you look at me
Love makes no sense
Love makes no sense

IITIIT
The way you look at me
sometimes it's so intense
Love makes no sense
It's just a mystery
I can't quite believe
Love makes no sense

FOUR-STEP CHORUSES

We know how to come up with chorus material, how to excavate a title, and where to position the title in a chorus. But how do we put those ideas together? How do we arrive at so many chorus possibilities from just a few chosen phrases?

I'm going to break down the process here using the same steps we used for verses.

Step 1. Destination-write with thoughts and feelings

The first step is to destination-write, beginning with one of your original sense-bound destination writings. For the chorus, this means focusing on thoughts and feelings instead of images and close detail.

Step 2. Parenthesize chorus phrases, and list potential titles

Next, reread the destination writing and parenthesize any phrases that resonate with you. Anything that pops out as a title contender will emerge at this point. Be sure to identify lines that can be shortened into two smaller phrases. Try to compile a list of ten or more phrases, then add them to the original external and internal columns.

Step 3. Look for rhyme pairs

Now just as we did with our initial verse content columns, look for rhymes between the new phrases. If you find you're lacking in rhyme, add in the internal column from the original destination writing. Then explore rhyme pairs between the external and new additions to the internal column.

Step 4. Choose a toggle pattern and rhyme scheme, and plug in phrases

Now you're ready to choose a toggling pattern and rhyme scheme and begin plugging in the phrases. Where you find you are missing a line to complete the toggle pattern or rhyme scheme, look to your existing phrases for content ideas. Remember that to sharpen the conversational quality of the chorus, we only need to employ those useful conjunctions and prepositions we talked about.

To practice the process of toggling, it's helpful to try your chorus with multiple toggling patterns. Try a four-line section, and then expand it to six lines. Try the title at the front and back, then only at the back. Add a seventh line to a six-line section just before the title repeats, or repeat the title as the seventh line at the end. Flexibility is the key, as you experiment with your phrases.

EXERCISE 7.2. Chorus Practice

Practice writing a few choruses of your own. Choose any destination writing and follow steps 1 through 4 of this chapter to write your chorus. Combine your phrases using any toggle pattern and rhyme scheme you feel produces the strongest chorus section.

LISTENING SUGGESTIONS
Sixpence None the Richer, "Kiss Me"
James Taylor, "Sweet Baby James"
Tim McGraw, "Something Like That"
Tom Petty, "Free Falling"

Chapter Summary

1. The function of the chorus is to give every tiny, experiential detail purpose and value.
2. The two types of choruses are abstract/metaphorical and list.
3. The three most common placements for the title are the first line, last line, and middle of the chorus.
4. The job of the line directly before the title is to set up the title.

CHAPTER 8

Contrast

THE BOREDOM BLOCKER

As you're toggling away, I'd like to take a moment to dwell on an important part of choosing a pattern and rhyme scheme. Whether we're aware of it or not, when we write, we choose a rhythm, a rhyme scheme, and a toggling pattern. Even when we drift creatively from section to section, we are settling on a length and pattern that just feels right. But what about those times when it doesn't feel right? What do we do when the song just isn't moving in the direction we'd like, and our audience has drifted back to their asparagus salad?

How we choose our toggle pattern doesn't have to be chance. In fact, it's often better if it isn't. When we take control over the structure our sections take, we also take control over their individuality. We can choose to make the sections sound identical in rhyme scheme, rhythm, and toggle pattern, or we can choose to create contrast between the song sections by structuring them differently. Varying these different aspects of a section yields freshness and new reason for our listeners to pay attention. That difference in structure is called "contrast." It tells our ears that new content is being delivered and refocuses our ability to receive the main purpose of the song. In short, it keeps us from becoming bored.

THE IMPORTANCE OF CONTRAST

Imagine if every section of a song had the same number of lines, the same rhyme scheme, the same rhythm, and the same toggling pattern. It would be predictable at best, and infinitely boring. Just as we can plan content using techniques like toggling, we can plan the structure of the song with contrast in mind.

There are a few ways to provide contrast. In this chapter, we'll focus on four major ways:

1. Changing the rhyme scheme
2. Changing the rhythm
3. Changing the number of lines
4. Changing the toggling pattern

I'm going to have to go back to my nursery rhyme about Mary and her little lamb. What if we were to write a new section that contrasted with the old? How would we ensure that it sound new and not just continue the monotony so far? Let's apply some techniques of contrast to design a chorus:

Mary had a little lamb
whose fleece was white as snow
and everywhere that Mary went
the lamb was sure to go

Laughing, playing
hiding, straying
no one ever had such fun
skipping, running
spinning, tumbling
friends as best as best friends come

What we have here is a six-line section. But you'll notice, as you read it down, that the rhythm has also changed. Beginning with line 1, the new rhythm provides an immediate signal that new material has arrived. The rhyme scheme has also changed. In the new section the scheme is AABCCB, contrasting with XAXA of the verse section. The combination of using both rhythm and rhyme creates a bolder contrast than just one of these tools alone.

The chorus is most often the point of highest intensity in a song. The melody often reaches its peak, the harmonies tend to settle onto their root forms, and whatever lyrical point we're driving at comes to a conclusion. When we choose our toggle patterns and rhyme schemes for the chorus section, we can deliberately choose those that contrast with the ones used in the verse and prechorus sections, optimizing the power given to our chorus. Very simply, if our verse consists of four lines, we might choose a six-line pattern for our chorus. If our verse consists of six lines followed by a two-line prechorus, our chorus might be a four-line pattern. Whatever we choose, it is only important that the new pattern brings freshness and renewed attention to the song.

CONTRAST AND TOGGLING

So let's see how these tools play out when we're planning our song structure. In chapter 5, we talked about how lyrics and music bond with phrasing. They are each made up of phrases that dictate rhyme and structure. When a musical phrase closes, the lyrical phrase should also close.

Consider a four-line section of EIEI. Let's say that section also has a rhyme scheme of ABAB. Let's also assume that section is a first verse.

Verse 1:
External Detail	A
Internal Detail	B
External Detail	A
Internal Detail	B

Now let's say we're going to write a prechorus that introduces a new topic. Our first inclination is to keep playing and singing with the same lovely rhythm and melody we've settled on for the first verse. However, we want to keep our audience on the edge of their seats, and a simple way to do that is to take them away from what's predictable. So, let's first try to change the number of lines of the section. We can choose any number of lines but four for the prechorus: either one, two, three, five, or even six lines. Since this section is supposed to create a build into the chorus, we probably don't want it longer than the verse, so let's choose either one, two, or three lines. Here's what we've got:

Verse 1:
External Detail	A
Internal Detail	B
External Detail	A
Internal Detail	B

Prechorus:

Line	?
Line	?
Line	?

Next, let's try altering the rhyme scheme and rhythm. Instead of ABA matching the first three lines of the verse, we'll choose AAA or AAB. We'll also change the rhythm of the lines to make sure they're shorter in length than those of the verse:

Prechorus:

Line Shortened	A
Line Shortened	A
Line Shortened	B

Last, let's choose a toggling pattern. Remember that the power position is often a thought or feeling line, so let's choose EEI or EII, IEI, or even III:

Prechorus:

Internal Detail	A
External Detail	A
Internal Detail	B

We can use the same process when it comes to the chorus and bridge. Only this time, we may be able to return to the four-line scheme for the chorus having had a prechorus to take our audience away from the predictable.

When we're creating contrast, it's important to remember that the *sooner* the variation occurs, the *stronger* the contrast will be. If we simply follow a verse of ABAB with a prechorus of ABA, the subtraction of a line won't appear to have any effect until the beginning of the omitted fourth line. But, if we follow that section of ABAB with two long lines of AA or three short lines of XAA, contrast begins immediately in that new section.

We don't have to employ all four ways simultaneously every time we want to achieve contrast. Just choosing one or two at a time can provide all the freshness we need to keep the song interesting.

The *sooner* the variation occurs, the *stronger* the contrast will be.

EXERCISE 8.1. Contrast in Action

Choose a toggling pattern for the new section that contrasts with the current pattern. Use any number or combination of the four ways to create contrast.

- Changing the rhyme scheme
- Changing the rhythm
- Changing the number of lines
- Changing the toggling pattern

Example 1

Verse 1:

External Detail	X
External Detail	A
External Detail	X
Internal Detail	A

⟶ **Prechorus:**

Chorus:

Internal Detail	A
Internal Detail	A
Title	T
Internal Detail	B
Internal Detail	B
Title	T

Example 2

Verse 1:

External Detail	X
External Detail	X
Internal Detail	A
External Detail	X
External Detail	X
Internal Detail	A

Prechorus:

Internal Detail Lengthened	A
Internal Detail Lengthened	A

⟶ **Chorus:**

Example 3

Chorus:

Title	T
Title	T
Internal Detail	X
Title	T

⟶ **Bridge:**

(Repeat Chorus)

LISTENING SUGGESTIONS

Ben Folds, "Still Fighting It"

Mike & the Mechanics, "The Living Years"

Brian Adams, "Summer of '69"

Marc Cohn, "Walking in Memphis"

Chapter Summary

1. There are four major ways to achieve contrast:
   - change the rhyme scheme
   - change the rhythm
   - change the number of lines
   - change the toggling pattern
2. The sooner the variation occurs, the stronger the contrast will be.

CHAPTER 9

The Content Compass

IDEAS THAT SIMPLIFY

So far, we've talked about how to grab our listeners with intense detail, and how to bring that detail to a point by writing a chorus that gives the detail value. We've also identified the critical power positions of song sections. In this chapter, we'll integrate steps 5, 8, and 9 into our 10-step process. These three steps involve the progression of the story. As we talk about the various options, we'll look for clues that help us decide which details belong where.

Step 1. Destination-write and create columns
Step 2. Find rhyme pairs
Step 3. Choose a rhyme scheme and toggling pattern
Step 4. Add prepositions and conjunctions
Step 5. Choose a plot progression
Step 6. Destination-write again using thought/feeling language
Step 7. Look for titles and write the chorus
Step 8. Write a second verse and prechorus
Step 9. Write the bridge
Step 10. Verbs, tense, point of view, and conversational quality

PYRAMIDING

Our first clue to organizing song content comes from a process I call "pyramiding."

Pyramiding describes the progression of a song idea from narrow to broad, from zoomed in to zoomed out. We can think of pyramiding in terms of our camera lens metaphor, or we can visualize the idea of pyramiding like the shape of a Christmas tree. Each section of the song utilizes pyramiding on a small scale, while the overall structure of the song utilizes pyramiding on a large scale.

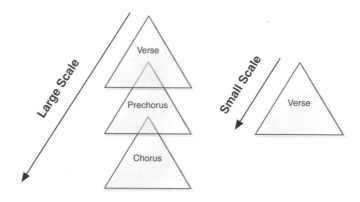

Imagine each of the three tiers was a song section with the top tier a verse, the middle tier a prechorus, and the bottom tier a chorus. We can see that the last line of each section is broader in scope than the first line of that section. This corresponds with the idea that the last line is an internal detail—a thought and feeling line. Its job is to zoom out and give all the previous detail value. We can also see that the title line, likely the lowest limb of the tree, is the broadest. As each section progresses, the scope of the song becomes broader, until the title line concludes the song purpose.

What this means for us as writers is some tricks we can keep up our sleeves. At every junction of our song sections, we can refer back to our tree and consider whether or not our content is moving in the tree-shaped direction. If at the ends of our sections, our content is refocusing to external detail, we are lacking the relationship of the detail to the main message of the song. Or if we begin a section with too much landscape in view, we are unable to broaden the content further by the end of the section, and we are not creating a strong enough experience. If our chorus seems to zoom in further than our verse sections, we may be having trouble convincing our listener it is the main message of the song. Keeping the tree shape in mind serves as a guide for the general and specific progressions of our song idea.

EXERCISE 9.1. Pyramiding in Action

Choose three of your favorite songs. Explain in your own words if and how pyramiding appears in the verse and chorus sections, as well as the overall shape of the song.

PLOT PROGRESSION

One placid morning in July, I was creeping along an L.A. freeway listening to the latest pop music hits. During one particular drive-time ditty, it occurred to me that I could actually use these songs to get out of the current writer's block I was in. Besides being catchy, they tend to use a format that has time and again proven to satisfy our structural needs. The content of each section can be summarized by a short description and applied to other ideas and still work. Though there are variations on these formats, they serve as excellent models from which to start building our own masterpieces.

Let's look at what this kind of content all boils down to.

Common Plot Progression

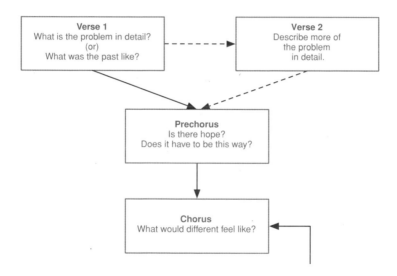

The second half of the song may go on to follow a format like this:

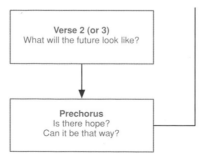

The bridge that typically follows, if there is one, often answers this question:

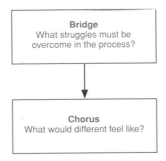

Now let's see how that applies to a song lyric.

"Breakaway"
by Bridget Benenate, Matthew Gerrard, Avril Lavigne

Verse 1:
Grew up in a small town
and when the rain would fall down
I'd just stare out my window
dreaming of what could be
and if I'd end up happy
I would pray

Verse 2:
Trying hard to reach out
But when I'd try to speak out
Felt like no one could hear me
Wanted to belong here
But something felt so wrong here
So I'd pray
I could break away

Chorus:
I'll spread my wings and I'll learn how to fly
I'll do what it takes 'til I touch the sky
And I'll make a wish
Take a chance
Make a change

And breakaway
Out of the darkness and into the sun
But I won't forget all the ones that I love
I'll take a risk
Take a chance
Make a change
And break away

Verse 3:
Wanna feel the warm breeze
Sleep under a palm tree
Feel the rush of the ocean
Get onboard a fast train
Travel on a jet plane, far away (I will)
And break away

[Chorus]

Bridge:
Buildings with a hundred floors
Swinging around revolving doors
Maybe I don't know where they'll take me but
Gotta keep moving on, moving on
Fly away, break away

[Chorus]

This first verse contains details about a specific event, time, or place. Those details are all focused around one central idea: mainly, the problem in detail.

After the first verse, we enter into the prechorus. These two lines are critical in setting up the chorus section content. They beg the question, "Is there hope? Does it have to be this way?" This is especially true of the last line of the prechorus, "I could break away."

The chorus then follows with a title describing what "different" would look like: "I'll spread my wings and I'll learn how to fly." The chorus section declares the answer to our prechorus question and describes what "different" would feel like.

Verses that follow the chorus in this type of plot progression often describe what the future will look like, involving more external detail. Here, Kelly Clarkson sings about what she desires for the future—how she visualizes the years ahead. Then the prechorus follows, asking again if it can indeed ever be that way. As we hit the chorus for the second time around, we've gained intensity, gathering a more detailed picture of what finally breaking away might look and feel like. The bridge section in this plot progression type provides contrast. It takes us off of our high for just a moment, examining the struggles that will have to be overcome. Bridges like these are especially powerful because they add new dimension to the chorus, exclaiming that no matter what the struggles, the singer will survive.

Whether following this song format exactly or just using it as a starting point to organize content, we can be assured that the verses will carry enough "evidence" to support the "claims" of our chorus. Furthermore, it can simplify the songwriting process and help keep our audience right there with us at every new idea.

There is another way we can describe the progression of our song content. We can focus on the element of "when." The most obvious use of "when" is the progression of each section of the song along a timeline. With this strategy, the first verse may describe an event, such as two people meeting and falling in love. The second verse may describe their wedding and the birth of their child. Then the last verse might progress to the child grown up, repeating the cycle of meeting and falling in love with someone else. This strategy is sometimes effective, but often falls short of creating a really believable experience for the listener. The amount of detail that can be included is small when so much time must pass within each section. What results is a sort of cookie-cutter lyric, predictable for the listener and yielding fewer original ideas for the writer.

A different strategy that I find more helpful is to consider the three time frames as an instigator for content: the past, the present, and the future. For example, I might begin my first verse about the future, describing the way my main character, or I, would like things to be. The chorus that follows might contrast that with a description of the present, the way things are. Then in the next verse I can move my main character back into the past, giving the listener background on where he/she/I came from. The chorus follows again with the way things are now. Finally in the bridge, I can make a more global statement about how things might start to change and become that future of which I dream. Ultimately, I only need to be aware of which time frame I have written my first verse in. Then, I can choose one of the other two time frames to move into for the next section.

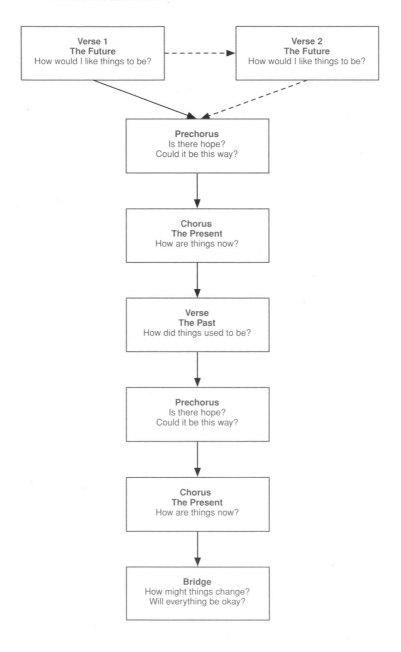

By using these progression possibilities as prompts, you can organize and pace your content for the greatest possible payoff.

In effective plot progressions, there is motive for writing the song that gives it purpose. Sometimes that motive is presented in the form of a problem that will be resolved. Sometimes that motive is presented as a contrast between the way things are and the way we'd like things to be. Either way, the contrast gives the song a more significant reason for having been born. It also gives our audience a significant reason to listen to what we have to say.

EXERCISE 9.2. Applying Plot Progressions

Decide how the plot progresses in each song below. Explain how that
particular progression is effective in connecting with the listener.

"How It Goes"

Verse 1:
So I'm standing in the place I started from
in the room I spent my life escaping from
with a painted dresser and a single bed
and curtains hanging like a high school prom dress

Verse 2:
Well I know I'm not the kid I used to be
but I wonder how I came so far from me
I didn't know that I was growing up
till I looked back and then the door was shut…but

> *Chorus:*
> *That's how it goes*
> *when you're fighting for survival*
> *yeah I guess that's just how it is*
> *when you're destined for something good*
> *but we kill ourselves*
> *trying to build ourselves*
> *into someone with something more*
> *when the truth is*
> *we were fine before*

Verse 3:
We grow up with a plan of what's gonna be
and we slowly come to terms with reality
then we get angry or we just go numb
and spend our thirties getting back to one…but

> *(Chorus)*

Bridge:
No I won't let these tears of mine
fall and forget where they go
With every year that passes by
I'll come further into my
into my own

(Chorus)

"When She Thinks About Leavin'"

Verse 1:
The TV is flashing
it blurs in the background
as she clears the plates off the table
and sighs at the dishes
then slips out a picture
taped by the cupboard door handle

Prechorus:
It's just sand, surf, and air
and she don't know where
she just likes how the waves seem to tumble

Chorus:
When she thinks about leaving
that's where she goes
to a place she can breathe
and the future's unknown
everyone needs somewhere far off to go
so she thinks about leaving
but that's all she needs to come home

Verse 2:
On Mondays thru Fridays
it's school books and lunch bags
and moving three kids to the bus stop
Then cell phone and briefcase
a kiss in the driveway
and watch while his car rounds the street block

Prechorus:
And it's all that she hoped
and it's less and it's more
but it's far from her own private Eden

Bridge:
Sometimes she clings to the sheets on their bed
and sinks in the place where he sleeps
and stares at the pictures of them and their kids
and feels so much joy that she weeps

(Repeat Chorus)

"Kaleidoscope"

Verse 1:
I went walking
late this evening
wondering if I should stay with you
and in the silence
of the streetlights
I figured out what I should do

Prechorus:
All of my life I've been changing
to what everyone wants me to be

Chorus:
But not anymore
I'm letting go
I'm not gonna be
a kaleidoscope
I'm saving my life
or what's left to lose
and taking it back from you
I was afraid
of some kind of change
but not anymore

Verse 2:
I was waiting
for life to happen
thought it began with someone else
I thought the answers
were somewhere out there
but they're inside of myself

> *Prechorus:*
> *You'd never believe all the colors*
> *that spun me and spun me around*

> *(Chorus)*

Verse 3:
Been shattered and scattered to pieces
denied them and lied they were me

> *(Chorus)*

FUNCTIONS OF THE SECOND VERSE

Many writers express difficulty when it comes to writing second verses and bridges. I have personally been known to avoid bridges at all costs, sparing myself the frustration of such a delicate section. But, sadly, sometimes they are needed, and that second verse after the first chorus—well, it's almost never optional.

A great benefit of staying detailed in the first verse is that everything hasn't already been said by the second verse. There is a whole world of places to explore after that first chorus, especially if we've stuck to a plot progression.

Second verses have some common characteristics we can revert back to whenever we're in doubt. They often contain a broader picture than the first verse.

Remember pyramiding on a large scale? Here's where it comes into play. Second verses zoom out in respect to first verses and are not necessarily set in specific events or time frames. Let's look at the difference between verses 1 and 2 below, of the song "Love Won't Take Chances."

Verse 1:

My dad proposed to Momma up at Fall Creek Falls
in one week they signed the papers down at City Hall
and Dad still likes to joke
he was too young then to know
but he still comes runnin' when she calls

(Chorus)

Verse 2:

I knew that you needed me to say it first
and I was still so mad I barely mouthed the words
But it's an incredible thing
what forgiveness brings
even when we've sunk down to our worst

This second verse contains more abstract material in lines 3 through 5 than verse 1. The first two lines just set the stage with "who" and "when." The second chorus will then take on deeper meaning, not because of any specific event that is described, but because of the internal thoughts and feelings that broaden the purpose of the song. As writers, by the second verse, we're sort of let off the hook in terms of including external detail. All those images in the first verse and the sense of "who," "where," and "when" have already created a framework from which our listener can relate to how we feel. As long as the first verse laid that strong foundation, we can ride on the wings of its connecting power.

Common Characteristics of Second Verses:
- More heavily internal
- Deepen the meaning of the chorus

Sometimes, the verse after the first chorus still continues external detail to refocus the listener's attention. In the song "When It's Over," this verse provides a snapshot of an event like the first and second verses, moving back in time and shedding more light on the story.

"When It's Over"

Verse 1:
There are trash cans by driveways
and lawn chairs in snow
there are Christmas lights hanging
from six weeks ago
there are dog barks and stalled cars
but all that I feel here is cold
I should go

> *Prechorus:*
> *but I'm stopped in your driveway*
> *the car in reverse*
> *and all I have to do*
> *is roll down to the curb but*

> *Chorus:*
> *I, I don't know much about walking away*
> *but I know when it's over*
> *and I, I don't know when love begins to change*
> *but I know when it's over*

Verse 2:
There was change on the dresser
there were clothes on the bed
there was nothing unusual
but that's how love gets
and we just let it go
until we couldn't save what was left
now here I am

> *Prechorus:*
> *I'm stopped in your driveway*
> *the car in reverse*
> *I don't want to leave*
> *but I don't want to hurt...'cuz*

> *(Chorus)*

By either moving to the past or the future for the second verse, we can add valuable information that will recolor the meaning of our next chorus. Following the plot progression strategy is one great way to achieve this.

FUNCTIONS OF THE BRIDGE

When it comes to bridges, we've really got to bring the message to a climax. The ultimate section to recolor, rekindle, rediscover, and unravel mystery is in that bridge. Here are a few common characteristics of bridges:

- Provide contrast using rhyme scheme, rhythm, number of lines, and/or toggling pattern with the other song sections
- Provide new meaning to the last chorus
- Resolve an issue or event within the content of the song

The bridge of "When It's Over" uses all of these characteristics to tie up the meaning of the song. It consists of two long lines, offers a new rhythm, utilizes a simple AA rhyme scheme, and provides new meaning to the song by saying that despite the pain, the singer has heart that someday the purpose will become clear:

Bridge:
I know that some things just run their course
and someday I'll know what the hurt was for

Whatever our story, the overall message of the bridge trumps that of the chorus and certainly the verses, leading the audience back into the last chorus like a caravan into the setting sun.

EXERCISE 9.3. Identifying Functions

In a single sentence, describe the functions of the bridge and verse after the first chorus of ten different songs. How do they adhere to the plot progressions in this chapter? How do they differ? How might you rewrite the progression of content to strengthen the song?

LISTENING SUGGESTIONS

Whitney Houston, "Didn't We Almost Have It All"

Michelle Branch, "Tuesday Morning"

Kelly Clarkson, "A Moment Like This"

Judds, "Love Can Build a Bridge"

Matchbox Twenty, "Real World"

Chapter Summary

1. Pyramiding describes the progression of a song idea from narrow to broad, from zoomed in to zoomed out.
2. We can use common plot progressions to orchestrate the content of our own songs.
3. The characteristics of a second verse are:
   - Utilizes internal detail
   - Deepens the meaning of the chorus
4. The characteristics of a bridge are:
   - Provides contrast
   - Provides new meaning to the last chorus
   - Resolves an issue or event within the content of the song

CHAPTER 10

Final Touches

THE FIRST DRAFT PHYSICAL

With so many ideas started, it's time to start getting accustomed to rewriting. The last step of our ten step process will fine-tune our lyric's ability to create a strong experience. We'll shift between different tenses and points of view, and improve the conversational quality of the lyric as easily as we change hats.

Step 1. Destination-write and create columns
Step 2. Find rhyme pairs
Step 3. Choose a rhyme scheme and toggling pattern
Step 4. Add prepositions and conjunctions
Step 5. Choose a plot progression
Step 6. Destination-write again using thought/feeling language
Step 7. Look for titles and write the chorus
Step 8. Write a second verse and prechorus
Step 9. Write the bridge
Step 10. Verbs, tense, point of view, and conversational quality

If you've been destination-writing every day, you have some great first drafts to work with. Here are some tools to oil the gears and take those drafts to the next level.

You already know from your destination writing that verbs hold the key to connection. You also know that each of the three elements of "who," "where," and "when" help to create connection in that first verse of your song. In this chapter, we'll look at how what you know can help you rewrite, and we'll also add in some exercises dealing with tense. Some simple alterations and the ability to stay flexible will shine all the dull areas.

VERBS GET ALL THE ACTION

In the first few chapters of this book, we talked about specific and generic verbs. Specific verbs have the ability to vault our listeners into our world, emotions and all. Generic verbs leave our audience disconnected—our tunes as memorable as what they ate last night for dinner.

As we rewrite, our goal will be to identify and strengthen each verb in the lyric. As you pass over each verb, consider whether it is helping to emphasize the emotion you want to evoke, or if it's just taking up space in the phrase.

EXERCISE 10.1. Verb Alternatives

For each phrase, find at least five verb alternatives that capture a stronger, more specific emotion.

Example:

Her whole body **moved** as she wept.
    Verb alternatives: Shook, pulsed, contracted, cringed, collapsed

You try it:

The door **closed** and I knew she was gone.
    Verb alternatives:

The cat's claws **stuck** to the carpet.
    Verb alternatives:

She **stooped** down to gather her dirty laundry.
    Verb alternatives:

Apply this process to your own songs by identifying each verb in your first drafts. Substitute some alternatives, and listen to the difference they make in the strength of your story.

POINT OF VIEW

Sometimes, we unconsciously assume a point of view when we write, but sometimes it is intentional. Whatever point of view we use—first person, direct address, or third person narrator—it should stay consistent throughout the song. You may find that you've used "he/she" in your first verse, and "you" in your prechorus. In effect, your role has changed from third person in verse 1 to direct address in the prechorus. The problem is that your audience is now unclear who the subject of the song is, and one of those three important elements is gone: "who." Anytime your audience is distracted by "how" you're singing, they're not paying attention to "what" you're singing. Making sure your role stays the same from the first line to the last ensures the greatest possibility of connection.

EXERCISE 10.2. Just One Point of View

Identify where the point of view changes in the lyrics below, and rewrite to correct the problem.

Example 1: "Love Won't Take Chances Anymore"

Verse:
My dad proposed to Momma up at Old Creek Falls
in one week they signed the papers down at City Hall
and Dad still likes to joke
he was too young then to know
but he still comes runnin' when she calls

Prechorus:
Sometimes I wonder
how you ever pulled through
when so many try
but few ever do

Example 2: "Colin's Song"

Verse 1:
Colin drove to Coney Island
and bought a ticket to a ride
thought he needed something violent
to scare him alive

Verse 2:
So you climbed into a boxcar
and watched the ground run out below
he was dying to feel something
out of control

TENSE

In chapter 6, we experimented with "when" and found that it plays an extremely critical role in helping our listener get on board with our story. That means that whatever tense we choose, we just need to stay consistent throughout the section. But tense offers another useful side effect outside of determining past, present, or future. Tense can offer flexibility, adding or taking away syllables to fit a melody or desired rhythm. Sometimes, more syllables are needed to match a melodic or rhythmic phrase, and playing with tense can stretch the line out to fill those spaces. Sometimes, changing the tense omits tongue-twisting prepositions and conjunctions. Each situation is different, so it's important to know your options.

In the following exercises, you'll be able to practice switching between tenses to achieve a different way of saying the same thing. Apply these different variations to your own lyrics, experimenting with past, present, and future.

EXERCISE 10.3. Playing with Tense

Rewrite each section below. If the section is in present tense, rewrite it in past tense and again in future tense. If the section is in past tense, rewrite it in future and again in present tense, etc.

*Hint: You may need to add a conjunction or preposition to make the tense work.

Section 1:

I was walking on the beach
with the sand under my feet
and the sky like a stage above my head

Present Tense:

Future Tense:

Possible Answers:

I walk on the beach (or) I will walk along the beach

Section 2:

When you told me you would leave
somewhere deep within my mind
I still didn't quite believe
you meant it this time

Present Tense:

Future Tense:

Possible Answers:

When you tell me you will leave
I still don't quite believe
you mean it this time

Section 3:

Sinking like a saucer
in a warm Egyptian sky
the sun lays down its armor
and gives in to the night

Past Tense:

Future Tense:

Possible Answers:

> *It sunk just like a saucer*
> *in a warm Egyptian sky*
> *the sun laid down its armor*
> *and gave in to the night*

Even better:

> *As the sun laid down its armor*
> *and gave in to the night*
> *it sunk just like a saucer*
> *in the warm Egyptian sky*

Chapter Summary

1. Exchanging specific verbs for generic verbs strengthens the experience for our listener.
2. Whatever the point of view, it should stay consistent throughout the song.
3. Whatever tense we choose, it should stay consistent throughout the section.

CHAPTER 11

Ten Steps to
Writing a Song

Throughout this book, you have learned various techniques to strengthen the experience you cause your listener. The more you write, the more easily you'll be able to incorporate these techniques into your lyrics.

In the following chapter, we'll review each step of our ten-step process. As we move through the steps, I'll develop a song using the techniques involved. In the beginning, you'll want to stick closely to this plan. Over time, you might find that you can integrate various steps and still naturally arrive at the effect you want. Let's get started.

TEN STEPS

Step 1. Destination-Write and Create Columns

This is the most important step of all. Take ten minutes and destination-write from either "where," "who," or "when." Make sure to stay focused on the six keys of connection:

sight	taste	smell
sound	touch	movement

*Hint: The more specific your verbs, the more sense-bound your object writing will be.

I have chosen to write from a "who" keyword, "hotel maid."

KEYWORD: `Hotel Maid (Verse)`

She comes around after the parties are over, after the romance of city lights and nightlife have died down and all that is left are the rumpled Kleenexes and mangled wrappers beside the beds and empty bottles left above the minibar. Her cart creaks as the wheels wobble down the hallway. Hair tied back in a neat bun, her apron starched and her stockings plunging into black loafers cushioning her exhausted arches, she refills the soaps, the toilet paper rolls, and the shower caps no one ever seems to really use. She drifts along unnoticed, unless her tiny knock interrupts some unsuspecting guest who barrels to the door and pounces it shut as if to say, "How dare you come in and try to do your job on my time?" Maids to us are like schoolteachers were when we were children. Without thinking we assume they simply disappear when evening falls, or actually live at the hotel where they lead hidden lives that revolve around bettering ours....

Step 2. Identify External and Internal/Create Rhyme Pairs

Draw a line down the center of a clean sheet of paper. At the top of the left column, write "External." At the top of the right column, write "Internal."

Then underline all the external phrases within your destination writing. Leave the internal phrases blank. Remember that external details provoke an image and internal phrases contain only a thought or feeling. Some phrases ride a thin line between external and internal. Just do the best you can, keeping in mind that the more specific the verb, the more acute the sense-bound action and the stronger the image.

<u>She comes around</u> after the parties are over, after the romance of <u>city lights</u> and <u>nightlife</u> have died

down and all that is left are the <u>rumpled Kleen-</u>
<u>exes</u> and <u>mangled wrappers</u> <u>beside the beds</u> and <u>empty</u>
<u>bottles</u> left <u>above the minibar</u>. Her <u>cart creaks</u> as
the <u>wheels wobble</u> <u>down the hallway</u>. <u>Hair tied back</u>
in a <u>neat bun</u>, her <u>apron starched</u> and her <u>stock-</u>
<u>ings plunging</u> into <u>black loafers</u> cushioning her
<u>exhausted arches</u>, she <u>refills the soaps</u>, the <u>toilet</u>
<u>paper rolls</u>, and the <u>shower caps</u> no one ever seems
to really use. She <u>drifts along unnoticed</u>, unless
her <u>tiny knock interrupts</u> some unsuspecting guest
who <u>barrels to the door</u> and <u>pounces it shut</u> as if to
say, "How dare you come in and try to do your job on
my time." Maids to us are like schoolteachers were
when we were children. Without thinking we assume
they simply disappear when evening falls, or actually live at the hotel where they lead hidden lives
that revolve around bettering ours....

Now, list your external phrases in the external column and your
favorite internal phrases in the internal column.

External		Internal
She comes around	apron startched	after the parties are
city lights	stockings plunging	over
nightlife	black loafers	after the romance
rumpled Kleenexes	exhausted arches	all that is left
mangled wrappers	refills the soaps	no one ever seems to
beside the beds	toilet paper rolls	really use
empty bottles	shower caps	maids are like school-
above the minibar	drifts along unnoticed	teachers
cart creaks	tiny knock interrupts	without thinking
wheels wobble	unsuspecting guest	assume they disap-
down the hallway	barrels to the door	pear
hair tied back	pounces it shut	when evening falls
neat bun		they live at the hotel
		lead hidden lives that
		revolve around
		ours

Look for rhyme pairs within and between the external and internal columns. The rhyme types from most closure to least are:

1. Perfect
2. Family
3. Additive/Subtractive
4. Assonance
5. Consonance

From my columns, I see that "bottle" and "wobble," "cart" and "minibar," "creaks" and "wheels" could be possible rhyme pairs. Look for rhymes between your external and internal columns as well. "Shower caps" and "hair tied back" could be structured as rhymed phrases within my section.

Step 3. Choose a Rhyme Scheme, Toggle Pattern, and Plot Progression

Begin thinking about a possible rhyme scheme and toggle pattern for each section. You may veer from that scheme as each section develops unique musical phrasing; however, keep in mind that contrast is key. For example, if you choose an ABAB rhyme scheme for your verse, you might choose an AABCCB scheme for your chorus. Even more simply put, if your verse is four lines long, try following it with a two-line prechorus and a six-line chorus. You can mix and match from the schemes and patterns below. Be sure to stick with one to two topics per four- and six-line section, using the inner lines to adequately expound on the topic(s).

Number of Lines	Toggle Pattern	Rhyme Scheme
2	EI	XX
	II	AA
4	EEEI	XAXA
	EIEI	ABAB
	IEII	AABB
6	EEIEEI	XXAXXA
	EIEEII	AABCCB
	IEIIEI	ABCABC

For my song, I choose a six-line verse followed by a four-line prechorus and a six-line chorus. My rhyme scheme and toggle pattern will be as follows:

	Toggling Pattern	**Rhyme Scheme**
Verse:	E	A
	I	X
	E	B
	E	A
	I	X
	E	B
Prechorus:	I	X
	E	A
	I	X
	I	A
Chorus:	Title	T
	Title	T
	Title	T
	I	A
	Variation on Title	T
	Title	T

Then review the plot progression questions, and choose a strategy to develop your story. Choose from these two common forms, including or omitting a second verse before the first chorus, and/or prechorus. Keep in mind that you may also choose a verse/refrain form. In this case, you might also try following any of the formats below through the first chorus. For example, the first verse/refrain would describe the problem in detail, the second verse/refrain would offer hope, and the third verse/refrain would describe the future as you'd like it to be. Another way to look at this is moving each verse/refrain chronologically forward in time so that the first verse is about the past, the second about the present, and the third about the future. Then try flipping verses 1 and 2, making the new verse 1 about the present and the new verse 2 reminiscing back to the past.

Plot Progression 1

Verse 1: What is the problem in detail/What was the past like?
Optional Verse 2: Describe more of the problem in detail.
Optional Prechorus: Can it be different/Does it have to be this way/

Is there hope?
Chorus: What would different feel like?
Bridge: What struggles must be overcome?

Plot Progression 2

Verse: The way things used to be/The way I'd like things to be
Prechorus: Is there hope?
Chorus: The way things are
Bridge: Everything's gonna be okay.

I choose the first common plot progression for my song.

Step 4. Toggle the Verse and Prechorus/ Add Conjunctions and Prepositions

Begin inserting external and internal phrases according to your rhyme scheme, until you have the skeleton of the section. Remember our three elements? Your first few lines should establish the "who," "when," and "where." You may not have all the rhymed phrases you need within your columns to complete a full section. In this case, insert any new ideas where needed. If you need an internal phrase that follows two external phrases, that internal phrase may simply be a comment on or feeling derived from those external lines. Don't worry about achieving the perfect phrasing, at this stage. Simply get a rough idea, using the details that best develop the story and allow us to connect with your subject.

Here are my phrases plugged into my chosen toggle pattern and rhyme scheme:

Verse:
She drifts along
after the parties are over
collects the trash and wrappers lying rumpled by the bed
hair tied back
her mind is far away
her cart creaks and wobbles down these lonely halls instead

I'm not completely satisfied with that last rhyme "instead." Remember that the last line of the section is the power position. Here, the limelight shines most brightly on my most forced rhyme. So I'll try a different configuration of my external and internal details. Feel free to go where the images take you, rearranging your toggling pattern as needed. Here I've used EEIEEI.

> *Verse:*
> *She drifts along*
> *collects the empty bottles*
> *after all the parties and the romance fade away*
> *She walks behind*
> *her cart creaks and wobbles*
> *disappears again until the next night turns to day*

There are many ways to write this same verse. The trick here is not to settle on something just because it took you three hours to construct. If you need time to be objective, put the verse away overnight and come back to it the next day with fresh ears. If you wrote one good section, you can do it again. Don't sacrifice content for rhyme.

Now I'll move on to my prechorus, a four-line section with a toggle pattern of IEII that poses the question, "Is there hope?"

> *Prechorus:*
> *She knows that she should hurry up and go*
> *tries to smooth her hair*
> *tired but she doesn't let it show*
> *she knows that there's*

Remember that the last line of the prechorus is also a power position and a great place for a thought or feeling line setting up or wrapping into the chorus.

When you add your conjunctions and prepositions, your goal will be to connect the phrases with conversational language. It can be as simple as adding conjunctions like "and" or "but," or filling in slightly with some internal language to complete the thought. Then take a step back and review your lyric so far. Read it once out loud. You might notice that your first verse is full of commas but lacking full phrases. Your lyrical phrasing should match the melodic phrasing. When a melodic phrase closes down, so should your lyrical phrase. Fragmented sentences and disjointed topics prevent your audience from sinking completely into your world. Revise any language that draws more attention to *how* it is said rather than *what* is said. Here's my lyric in a more conversational form:

Verse:
She drifts along
and collects the empty bottles
after all the parties and the romance fade away
She walks behind
a cart that creaks and wobbles
and disappears again until the next night turns to day

Prechorus:
She knows that she should hurry up and go
so she tries to smooth her hair
and she's tired but she doesn't let it show
'cuz she knows that there's

Step 5. Destination-Write Again Using Thought/Feeling Language

You're looking for titles and chorus material this time. Destination-write again, only this time, talk about your thoughts and feelings. Start by reading through your original destination writing and begin where you left off, speaking from the mind of your main character. Here goes:

KEYWORD: Hotel Maid (Chorus)

She's unappreciated. No one knows she exists. I wonder what she thinks about when she cleans my room. Does she think of all the choices she made that brought her here? And does she think of all the struggles she's overcome just to get here? I wish she knew how I respect her, how I think the world of what she does for me. She doesn't know it, but oh how she humbles me. Does her boss treat her well, or does he despise his own reflection when he speaks to her? I wonder if she'll ever find her way out, climb past the invisible line that's holding her down....

Step 6. Look for Titles and Rhyme Pairs/Write the Chorus

By writing with internal language, I can find more thoughts and feelings that might be good title material. From my paragraph, I like the sound of "an invisible line she can't seem to cross." I also like the metaphor of an invisible line for a race, a status, or a financial position that is difficult to rise above. So with that in mind, I'll write towards the title, "Invisible Line." Follow your toggling pattern and write the chorus, positioning your rhymed phrases in the appropriate positions in the scheme. Remember the bodyguard and power position. Add conjunctions and prepositions.

I'll use repetition to come up with a simple chorus around my title, "Invisible Line":

Chorus:
A line
invisible line
invisible line
she'll get by
there's a line
invisible line

Now I'll add appropriate conversational conjunctions and prepositions:

Chorus:
A line
an invisible line
an invisible line
that someday she'll get by
there's a line
an invisible line

*Hint: Try exchanging the tense of your verbs. For example, "She drifts along *collecting* empty bottles" instead of "...*collects* empty bottles." Keep the verb forms consistent throughout your verse. I chose not to do that here because in line 5, "creaks and wobbles" would become "creaking and wobbling," throwing off the rhythm of the lyric.

Step 7. Construct the Second Verse and Prechorus

Follow the chosen plot progression, and use pyramiding to write your second verse and prechorus. Use the toggling pattern of your first verse, but feel free to involve more internal detail this time. You may choose to use the same prechorus or write a new one. Add conjunctions and prepositions.

Here is my second verse followed by a second prechorus:

Verse:
She sits alone
and she watches through the window
as the city bus collects and spits her out onto her street
She's finally home
and flips her shoes off on the floor
her burning heels are screaming and she needs to get some sleep

Prechorus:
But she knows that she should hurry up and go
'cuz the night shift's starting soon
and she's tired but she doesn't let it show
so she tries her best to move

Step 8. Construct the Bridge

Follow your plot progression and pyramiding to toggle a bridge. Choose a toggling pattern that contrasts with your chorus and verse for maximum effect. Consider how your section will add new meaning to the last chorus. Add conjunctions and prepositions.

Here is my bridge, written around the idea of what struggles must be overcome:

Bridge:
Someday she'll defeat the odds
break the walls and ceilings down
and she won't have to fight anymore

Step 9. Verbs, Tenses, and Points of View

Check the tense and the point of view of your lyric. Have you switched between first and third person? Is the tense consistent throughout each section? Review your lyric once more, and circle all the verbs. Consider whether there are more specific verbs that accurately describe the action taking place. The closer you zoom in, the more specific the detail and stronger the experience. Refer to your thesaurus for better word choices.

Verse:

She drifts along

and collects the empty bottles

after all the parties and the romance fade away

She walks behind

a cart that creaks and wobbles

and disappears again until the next night turns to day

My weakest verb here is "walks." So I'll go to my thesaurus for more choices. Since I want the back half of my section to match up with the front half, I need a one-syllable word to replace "walks." That limits my options to a few good words like "slips," "slides," "steps," or maybe "rolls." In this instance, I'll choose "slides." Repeat this search for every verb that isn't pulling its weight within your section.

Step 10. Check Conversational Quality

Read through your lyric out loud. Are there any fragmented phrases? Can you exchange conjunctions and prepositions to better connect phrases? Do "who," "where," and "when" all appear within the first few lines of the song? Rewrite where needed.

Here is my finished lyric:

Verse 1:
She drifts along
and collects the empty bottles
after all the parties and romance fade away
She slides behind
a cart that creaks and wobbles
and disappears again until the next night turns to day

> *Prechorus:*
> *She knows that she should hurry up and go*
> *so she tries to smooth her hair*
> *and she's tired but she doesn't let it show*
> *'cuz she knows that there's*

> > *Chorus:*
> > *A line*
> > *an invisible line*
> > *an invisible line*
> > *that someday she'll get by*
> > *there's a line*
> > *an invisible line*

Verse 2:
She sits alone
and she watches through the window
as the city bus collects and spits her out onto her street
She's finally home
and flips her shoes off on the floor
her burning heels are screaming and she needs to get some sleep

> *Prechorus:*
> *But she knows that she should hurry up and go*
> *'cuz the night shift's starting soon*
> *and she's tired but she doesn't let it show*
> *so she tries her best to move*

> > *Chorus:*
> > *A line*
> > *an invisible line*

an invisible line
that someday she'll get by
there's a line
an invisible line

> *Bridge:*
> *Someday she'll defeat the odds*
> *break the walls and ceilings down*
> *and she won't have to fight anymore*

Chorus:
A line
an invisible line
an invisible line
that someday she'll get by
there's a line
an invisible line

Afterword

I hope that you find this process useful in developing your own ideas into songs you love. With persistence and dedication, you will see great improvement in your writing. What's even more exciting is the fingerprint that will emerge as you expose your life through strong experiences. There isn't and never will be another songwriter like you, as long as you use your strength—your unique perspective. With it, you can look forward to a lifetime of fresh ideas and dedicated audiences. But most of all, you can be satisfied that you brought something worthwhile into the world—yourself.

—Andrea Stolpe

Destination Writing Keywords

PEOPLE, PLACES, AND TIMES

"Who"

barmaid
policeman
middle-aged woman
diplomat
shopaholic
construction worker
priest

actor
BMW driver on his
  cell phone
hang glider
Olympic swimmer
orphan
widow
architect

chain smoker
drug addict
family business
  owner
hairdresser
dentist
husband and father
  of four

"When"

just after midnight
while brushing your
  teeth
pulling into your
  driveway
just before falling
  asleep

just waking up
driving to work in the
  morning
while waiting for test
  results
just after a kiss

while putting on
  makeup
while running the
  garbage disposal
running through the
  airport
just before a car crash

"Where"

coffee shop
police station
inside a stolen car
a hotel room
unemployment line
a library
alley in NYC

airport
on the interstate
a wine cellar
a school gym
an office cubicle
on top of Mt. Everest
standing in front of
    the open
    refrigerator

your bedroom
the last pew of a
    church
the bottom of the
    Grand Canyon
your living room with
    the lights out
a fine art gallery
gazing through a
    bakery window in
    the rain

Prepositions and Conjunctions

Prepositions show relationships between nouns and pronouns and other words in terms of space, time, and other senses. Listed below are useful prepositions for our songs.

about	behind	in	out
above	beneath	in spite of	out of
across	beside	inside	through
after	between	instead of	to
along	beyond	like	toward
among	by	near	under
around	during	next to	until
at	except for	of	up
because of	for	on	upon
before	from	onto	with

Conjunctions connect words, phrases, and clauses. Listed below are useful conjunctions for our songs.

after	even though	since	until
although	for	so	when
and	if	so that	whenever
as	in order that	than	where
as if	once	that	wherever
as though	or	though	while
because	rather than	unless	yet
before			
but			
even if			

About the Author

Jonathan David Photography

Andrea Stolpe is a performing artist, songwriter, and educator. Throughout her career, she has worked as a staff writer for EMI, Almo-Irving, and Universal Music Publishing, and her songs have been recorded by Faith Hill, Daniel Lee Martin, and others. She is the author of the online course *Commercial Songwriting Techniques*, part of Berkleemusic's songwriting program. Andrea continues to tour as a solo artist and lead songwriting workshops around the country. She currently lives in Los Angeles with her husband, Producer and Recording Engineer Jan Stolpe.

Select songs Andrea used as examples in this book are recorded on her CD *Breaking Even*. Order it from her Web site www.andreastolpe.com, where you will also find additional songwriting resources.

INDEX

More Fine Publications

GUITAR

BLUES GUITAR TECHNIQUE
by Michael Williams
50449623 Book/Online Audio $27.99

BERKLEE GUITAR CHORD DICTIONARY
by Rick Peckham
50449546 Jazz – Book $14.99
50449596 Rock – Book.....................$12.99

BERKLEE GUITAR STYLE STUDIES
by Jim Kelly
00200377 Book/Online Media............$24.99

CLASSICAL TECHNIQUE FOR THE MODERN GUITARIST
by Kim Perlak
00148781 Book/Online Audio..............$19.99

CONTEMPORARY JAZZ GUITAR SOLOS
by Michael Kaplan
00143596 Book.................................$16.99

COUNTRY GUITAR STYLES
by Mike Ihde
00254157 Book/Online Audio.............$24.99

CREATIVE CHORDAL HARMONY FOR GUITAR
by Mick Goodrick and Tim Miller
50449613 Book/Online Audio $22.99

FUNK/R&B GUITAR
by Thaddeus Hogarth
50449569 Book/Online Audio $19.99

GUITAR SWEEP PICKING
by Joe Stump
00151223 Book/Online Audio...............$19.99

JAZZ GUITAR FRETBOARD NAVIGATION
by Mark White
00154107 Book/Online Audio $22.99

JAZZ GUITAR IMPROVISATION STRATEGIES
by Steven Kirby
00274977 Book/Online Audio............$24.99

JAZZ SWING GUITAR
by Jon Wheatley
00139935 Book/Online Audio............$24.99

MODAL VOICINGS FOR GUITAR
by Rick Peckham
00151227 Book/Online Media $24.99

A MODERN METHOD FOR GUITAR*
by William Leavitt
Volume 1: Beginner
00137387 Book/Online Video..............$24.99
*Other volumes, media options, and supporting songbooks available.

A MODERN METHOD FOR GUITAR SCALES
by Larry Baione
00199318 Book.................................$14.99

TRIADS FOR THE IMPROVISING GUITARIST
by Jane Miller
00284857 Book/Online Audio............$22.99

BASS

BASS LINES
Fingerstyle Funk
by Joe Santerre
50449542 Book/Online Audio $19.99
Metal
by David Marvuglio
00122465 Book/Online Audio $19.99
Rock
by Joe Santerre
50449478 Book/Online Audio $22.99

BERKLEE JAZZ BASS
by Rich Appleman, Whit Browne, and Bruce Gertz
50449636 Book/Online Audio $22.99

FUNK BASS FILLS
by Anthony Vitti
50449608 Book/Online Audio............$22.99

INSTANT BASS
by Danny Morris
50449502 Book/CD $9.99

READING CONTEMPORARY ELECTRIC BASS
by Rich Appleman
50449770 Book...............................$22.99

VOICE

BELTING
by Jeannie Gagné
00124984 Book/Online Media $22.99

THE CONTEMPORARY SINGER
by Anne Peckham
50449595 Book/Online Audio $27.99

JAZZ VOCAL IMPROVISATION
by Mili Bermejo
00159290 Book/Online Audio $19.99

TIPS FOR SINGERS
by Carolyn Wilkins
50449557 Book/CD.........................$19.95

VOCAL WORKOUTS FOR THE CONTEMPORARY SINGER
by Anne Peckham
50448044 Book/Online Audio...........$24.99

YOUR SINGING VOICE
by Jeannie Gagné
50449619 Book/Online Audio $29.99

WOODWINDS/BRASS

TRUMPET SOUND EFFECTS
by Craig Pederson and Ueli Dörig
00121626 Book/Online Audio................$14.99

TECHNIQUE OF THE SAXOPHONE
by Joseph Viola
50449820 Volume 1......................$19.99
50449830 Volume 2......................$22.99
50449840 Volume 3......................$22.99

PIANO/KEYBOARD

BERKLEE JAZZ KEYBOARD HARMONY
by Suzanna Sifter
00138874 Book/Online Audio $29.99

BERKLEE JAZZ PIANO
by Ray Santisi
50448047 Book/Online Audio $22.99

BERKLEE JAZZ STANDARDS FOR SOLO PIANO
Arranged by Robert Christopherson, Hey Rim Jeon, Ross Ramsay, Tim Ray
00160482 Book/Online Audio.............$19.99

CHORD-SCALE IMPROVISATION FOR KEYBOARD
by Ross Ramsay
50449597 Book/CD.......................$19.99

CONTEMPORARY PIANO TECHNIQUE
by Stephany Tiernan
50449545 Book/DVD $29.99

HAMMOND ORGAN COMPLETE
by Dave Limina
00237801 Book/Online Audio $24.99

JAZZ PIANO COMPING
by Suzanne Davis
50449614 Book/Online Audio $22.99

LATIN JAZZ PIANO IMPROVISATION
by Rebecca Cline
50449649 Book/Online Audio $29.99

SOLO JAZZ PIANO
by Neil Olmstead
50449641 Book/Online Audio............$42.99

DRUMS/PERCUSSION

BEGINNING DJEMBE
by Michael Markus and Joe Galeota
00148210 Book/Online Video..............$16.99

BERKLEE JAZZ DRUMS
by Casey Scheuerell
50449612 Book/Online Audio............$24.99

DRUM SET WARM-UPS
by Rod Morgenstein
50449465 Book................................$14.99

DRUM STUDIES
by Dave Vose
50449617 Book................................$12.99

A MANUAL FOR THE MODERN DRUMMER
by Alan Dawson and Don DeMichael
50449560 Book................................$14.99

MASTERING THE ART OF BRUSHES
by Jon Hazilla
50449459 Book/Online Audio.............$19.99

PHRASING: ADVANCED RUDIMENTS FOR CREATIVE DRUMMING
by Russ Gold
00120209 Book/Online Media $19.99

WORLD JAZZ DRUMMING
by Mark Walker
50449568 Book/CD $22.99

Berklee Press publications feature material developed at the Berklee College of Music.
To browse the complete Berklee Press Catalog, go to **www.berkleepress.com**

STRINGS/ROOTS MUSIC

BERKLEE HARP
Chords, Styles, and Improvisation for Pedal and Lever Harp
by Felice Pomeranz
00144263 Book/Online Audio.............$24.99

BEYOND BLUEGRASS
Beyond Bluegrass Banjo
by Dave Hollander and Matt Glaser
50449610 Book/CD $19.99

Beyond Bluegrass Mandolin
by John McGann and Matt Glaser
50449609 Book/CD $19.99

Bluegrass Fiddle and Beyond
by Matt Glaser
50449602 Book/CD $19.99

CONTEMPORARY CELLO ETUDES
by Mike Block
00159292 Book/Online Audio..............$19.99

EXPLORING CLASSICAL MANDOLIN
by August Watters
00125040 Book/Online Media $24.99

FIDDLE TUNES ON JAZZ CHANGES
by Matt Glaser
00120210 Book/Online Audio..............$16.99

THE IRISH CELLO BOOK
by Liz Davis Maxfield
50449652 Book/Online Audio $27.99

JAZZ UKULELE
by Abe Lagrimas, Jr.
00121624 Book/Online Audio $22.99

BERKLEE PRACTICE METHOD

GET YOUR BAND TOGETHER
With additional volumes for other instruments, plus a teacher's guide.
Bass
by Rich Appleman, John Repucci, and the Berklee Faculty
50449427 Book/CD $24.99
Drum Set
by Ron Savage, Casey Scheuerell, and the Berklee Faculty
50449429 Book/CD $17.99
Guitar
by Larry Baione and the Berklee Faculty
50449426 Book/CD $19.99
Keyboard
by Russell Hoffmann, Paul Schmeling, and the Berklee Faculty
50449428 Book/Online Audio $14.99

MUSIC BUSINESS

CROWDFUNDING FOR MUSICIANS
by Laser Malena-Webber
00285092 Book...........................$17.99

HOW TO GET A JOB IN THE MUSIC INDUSTRY
by Keith Hatschek with Breanne Beseda
00130699 Book...........................$27.99

MAKING MUSIC MAKE MONEY
by Eric Beall
00355740 Book...........................$29.99

MUSIC LAW IN THE DIGITAL AGE
by Allen Bargfrede
00366048 Book...........................$24.99

PROJECT MANAGEMENT FOR MUSICIANS
by Jonathan Feist
50449659 Book...........................$34.99

THE SELF-PROMOTING MUSICIAN
by Peter Spellman
00119607 Book...........................$24.99

MUSIC THEORY/EAR TRAINING/IMPROVISATION

BEGINNING EAR TRAINING
by Gilson Schachnik
50449548 Book/Online Audio $17.99

THE BERKLEE BOOK OF JAZZ HARMONY
by Joe Mulholland and Tom Hojnacki
00113755 Book/Online Audio..............$29.99

BERKLEE CORRESPONDENCE COURSE
00244533 Book/Online Media...........$29.99

BERKLEE EAR TRAINING DUETS AND TRIOS
by Gaye Tolan Hatfield
00284897 Book/Online Audio...........$19.99

BERKLEE MUSIC THEORY
by Paul Schmeling
50449615 **Rhythm, Scales Intervals** $24.99
50449616 **Harmony**....................$24.99

CONDUCTING MUSIC TODAY
by Bruce Hangen
00237719 Book/Online Video.............$24.99

IMPROVISATION FOR CLASSICAL MUSICIANS
by Eugene Friesen with Wendy M. Friesen
50449637 Book/CD $24.99

JAZZ DUETS
by Richard Lowell
00302151 C Instruments....................$14.99

MUSIC NOTATION
by Mark McGrain
50449399 Theory and Technique....$24.99

REHARMONIZATION TECHNIQUES
by Randy Felts
50449496 Book..........................$29.99

MUSIC PRODUCTION & ENGINEERING

AUDIO MASTERING
by Jonathan Wyner
50449581 Book/CD........................$29.99

AUDIO POST PRODUCTION
by Mark Cross
50449627 Book...........................$19.99

CREATING COMMERCIAL MUSIC
by Peter Bell
00278535 Book/Online Media $19.99

THE SINGER-SONGWRITER'S GUIDE TO RECORDING IN THE HOME STUDIO
by Shane Adams
00148211 Book/Online Audio..............$19.99

UNDERSTANDING AUDIO
by Daniel M. Thompson
00148197 Book...........................$42.99

WELLNESS/AUTOBIOGRAPHY

LEARNING TO LISTEN: THE JAZZ JOURNEY OF GARY BURTON
00117798 Book...........................$34.99

MANAGE YOUR STRESS AND PAIN THROUGH MUSIC
by Dr. Suzanne B. Hanser and Dr. Susan E. Mandel
00117798 Book...........................$34.99

MUSICIAN'S YOGA
by Mia Olson
50449587 Book...........................$19.99

THE NEW MUSIC THERAPIST'S HANDBOOK
by Suzanne B. Hanser
00279325 Book...........................$29.99

SONGWRITING/COMPOSING/ARRANGING

ARRANGING FOR HORNS
by Jerry Gates
00121625 Book/Online Audio.............$22.99

ARRANGING FOR STRINGS
by Mimi Rabson
00190207 Book/Online Audio............$22.99

BEGINNING SONGWRITING
by Andrea Stolpe with Jan Stolpe
00138503 Book/Online Audio $22.99

BERKLEE CONTEMPORARY MUSIC NOTATION
by Jonathan Feist
00202547 Book...........................$24.99

COMPLETE GUIDE TO FILM SCORING
by Richard Davis
50449607 ....$34.99

CONTEMPORARY COUNTERPOINT
by Beth Denisch
00147050 Book/Online Audio............$24.99

COUNTERPOINT IN JAZZ ARRANGING
by Bob Pilkington
00294301 Book/Online Audio............$24.99

THE CRAFT OF SONGWRITING
by Scarlet Keys
00159283 Book/Online Audio..............$22.99

CREATIVE STRATEGIES IN FILM SCORING
by Ben Newhouse
00242911 Book/Online Media............$27.99

ESSENTIAL SONGWRITING
by Jonathan Feist & Jimmy Kachulis
50448051 ....$10.99

JAZZ COMPOSITION
by Ted Pease
50448000 Book/Online Audio $39.99

MELODY IN SONGWRITING
by Jack Perricone
50449419 Book..........................$24.99

MODERN JAZZ VOICINGS
by Ted Pease and Ken Pullig
50449485 Book/Online Audio...........$24.99

MUSIC COMPOSITION FOR FILM AND TELEVISION
by Lalo Schifrin
50449604 Book..........................$39.99

MUSIC NOTATION
50449540 **Preparing Scores & Parts**....$24.99
50449399 **Theory and Technique**...........$24.99

POPULAR LYRIC WRITING
by Andrea Stolpe
50449553 Book..........................$16.99

SONGWRITING: ESSENTIAL GUIDE
by Pat Pattison
50481582 **Lyric and Form Structure** $19.99
00124366 **Rhyming** $22.99

SONGWRITING IN PRACTICE
by Mark Simos
00244545 Book..........................$16.99

SONGWRITING STRATEGIES
by Mark Simos
50449621 Book..........................$24.99

THE SONGWRITER'S WORKSHOP
by Jimmy Kachulis
50449519 **Harmony** $29.99
50449518 **Melody** $24.99

Prices subject to change without notice. Visit your local music dealer or bookstore, or go to **halleonard.com** to order

YOUR RESOURCE FOR THEORY, EAR TRAINING, and Improvisation

berklee press

Berklee Music Theory – 2nd Edition

by Paul Schmeling

This essential method features rigorous, hands-on, "ears-on" practice exercises that help you explore the inner working of music, presenting notes, scales, and rhythms as they are heard in pop, jazz, and blues. Book 2 focuses on harmony, including triads, seventh chords, inversions, and voice leading.

50449615 Book 1 – Book/CD Pack $24.99
50449616 Book 2 – Book/CD Pack $22.99

A Guide to Jazz Improvisation

by John LaPorta
Book/CD Pack

First published in 1968 and now thoroughly updated and revised, John LaPorta's method provides a practical and intuitive approach to teaching basic jazz improvisation through 12 lessons and an accompanying CD.

50449439 C Instruments $19.95
50449441 B♭ Instruments $19.99
50449442 E♭ Instruments $19.99
50449443 BC Instruments $19.99

Improvisation for Classical Musicians
strategies for creativity and expression

by Eugene Friesen with Wendy M. Friesen

Features concepts and exercises that foster the creative mindset and help classical performers acquire the technical tools necessary for improvisation, including: playing by ear, applying music theory to instruments, and more. The accompanying recording includes demonstration and play-along tracks.

50449637 Book/CD Pack.....................................$24.99

Prices, contents, and availability subject to change without notice.

Essential Ear Training for the Contemporary Musician

by Steve Prosser

This method teaches musicians to hear the music they are seeing, notate the music they have composed or arranged, develop their music vocabulary, and understand the music they are hearing. The book features a complete course with text and musical examples, and studies in rhythm, sight recognition, sol-fa, and melody.

50449421..$16.95

Music Notation
preparing scores and parts

by Matthew Nicholl and Richard Grudzinski

Teaches: how to create scores that are easy to conduct and parts that are easy to perform; standards for handwritten vs. computer-generated scores; common practices; publication standards; and more.

50449540..$16.95

Jazz Improvisation: A Personal Approach
with Joe Lovano

Play any instrument with more spontaneity and feeling. Develop your own voice with the practical techniques that have helped make Joe Lovano one of the most respected improvisers of our time. 59 minutes.

50448033 DVD...$19.95

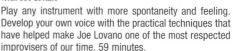
berklee press

EXCLUSIVELY DISTRIBUTED BY

HAL•LEONARD® CORPORATION

7777 W. BLUEMOUND RD. P.O. BOX 13819 MILWAUKEE, WI 53213

www.halleonard.com

0613